To Bin

[signature]

Entombed In
ALCATRAZ

3-24-12

Published by:
Robert Victor Luke
Co-Publisher Ida Marie Luke

All family photographs property of: Robert Victor Luke
Other photographs used with permission of Ida Marie Luke,
Ian Craig, and Timothy Brazil.

ISBN 978-0-578-08295-0

Cover Design by: Timothy Brazil and Robert Luke
Aided by *the*BookDesigners
Interior Design by: *the*BookDesigners

Entombed In
ALCATRAZ

An Autobiography
by
Robert Luke #1118AZ

Dedicated to

Ida Marie Luke

My

Best friend
Golfing buddy
Fishing buddy
Cheerleader
And marvelous wife of 37 years,
who urged me to write this book.
And without whose help this book could
not have been written.

Thank you

Robert Luke

Acknowledgements

Alcatraz National Park Service Rangers
and employees

Especially Rangers
John Cantwell
Lori Brosnan
Al Blank

Also
Bill Duckett-for his friendship and support
Ian Craig-video photographer
Tim Brazil-video photographer
Ana Brazil-proofreader
Steve McDonald-video photographer
Joseph Sanchez-National Archives

And

Michael Esslinger-Alcatraz
Historian and Author

Table of Contents

Preface

Alcatraz was certainly no myth. Alcatraz was THE maximum security federal penitentiary of the time. All of the men who were there (guards and prisoners) from 1934 to 1963 can attest to that. Alcatraz was harsh reality! Living hell for some, and just another prison for others.

There were a total of 1,538 prisoners incarcerated in Alcatraz, and each one has a different memory of the time he served on 'the Rock'. But one thing is truth and reality: all the men who were prisoners on Alcatraz were the dregs of society. I believe this, even though I was one of them, and even though some of us changed our lives.

This book was written with the recollections of the author and data from the National Archives. Some parts may not be accurate, and may be only the memories of an old man.

Perhaps this autobiography can explain why the mystery became a myth, or did the myth become a mystery? Let the reader be the judge.

Chapter One
April 14, 1954

THE PASSENGER TRAIN pulled into the Richmond, California station early in the morning. One of the cars was a prison car with barred, screened, and blacked out windows. There were several prisoners in the car, and I was one of them.

We had made a two day and one night journey from Leavenworth Federal Penitentiary in Kansas. I was shackled, my left ankle to the right ankle of another prisoner, and I don't remember who he was. We were also separately handcuffed. We were fed some kind of boxed food twice a day, with water to drink. This was not a sleeper car, so we sat up for the complete trip. There was one toilet at one end of the car, and it was awkward using the facility while being shackled to another prisoner, but we managed. We had to first get permission from the federal marshal who sat behind a screened area in the front of the car. But we had all been in prisons before and knew there was no privacy to be expected. There were several marshals on the train, separated by heavy screens, and they were armed.

Soon the outer door and then the inner screened door opened, and several men in black uniforms and hats came into the car. They were Alcatraz Prison guards. They checked our handcuffs and leg irons, and then we were moved out of the car two by two onto the station platform. It was an ungainly process and we had to be helped. When I got onto the platform I realized we were on the opposite side of the train from the station. There were a lot of uniformed police officers present and most of them were carrying shotguns.

We walked a short distance away to a dock where a boat was tied up. It was the Warden Johnson, the Alcatraz prison boat, named after the first warden of Alcatraz. It was a cool, sunny morning, and we were only wearing coveralls, slippers, and light coats. I, for one, felt the chill. We were finally all aboard the Warden Johnson and started moving away from the dock out into San Francisco Bay, and headed west toward the Golden Gate Bridge.

I had recognized where we were because in 1945, when I was in the US Navy, I had caught my first ship not far from here, in Alameda. We proceeded across the bay and on our left could see the Bay Bridge and in the distance, San Francisco. Soon, Treasure Island was on our left and I remembered being there for three weeks before I boarded my first ship, the APA 149 Audabon, a troop transport. Next was Yerba Buena Island where I had a General Court Marshall for going AWOL in 1948. In those four years I had probably passed Alcatraz about six times. It's too bad that I didn't have some kind of premonition of this day on my way out to Alcatraz!

I couldn't see Alcatraz until the Warden Johnson made a long, slow turn toward the dock. Then I could see the prison on top of the island with several buildings down near the water and the dock. My first impression of Alcatraz was of a French chateau, but I immediately realized this was no country home, but was to be my prison for several years.

We reached the dock and soon the boat was secured. Then we were unloaded with some difficulty and loaded into a small bus. We went up a narrow, winding, steep road to what I later learned was the basement of the prison. On the way up I couldn't help looking at the bay and San Francisco and wondering when I would see them again. All the prisoners and guards had been quiet on the boat out to Alcatraz and the ride up the hill. Each lost in his own thoughts. Anxiety, fear, and apprehension were also riding up that hill with us.

The guards helped us off the bus and we went through two heavy barred gates and into a small area, turned left, and entered a large room. It was the shower room. About 100 by 50 feet with shower heads running down the middle of the room about four feet apart. There were no shower stalls, but as I said before, men have been taking communal showers and having other bodily functions in high school, the armed services and other places all their lives. On the right there was a screened enclosure with bins of clothes and other items.

We were lined up along the far wall across from the entrance to the shower room. Then the guards removed our handcuffs and shackles, told us to strip and put everything in front of us on the floor. I was glad to get the shackles off, because no matter how careful we were, my ankle was raw and sore. All the clothes were searched, then picked up and put into a large wheeled laundry basket.

We were then strip searched, including all cavities. A medical person gave us a cursory physical examination, consisting of asking us how we felt. He got back a lot of "ok's." Then we were all given a bar of rough soap, a towel and we got to take a hot shower. It felt like I was not only washing away the dirt and grime of the trip from Leavenworth, but was being made ready for whatever happened next. After we dried off we were issued shorts, t-shirts, denim pants, shirts, shoes, and socks. Also, I seem to remember Navy pea coats and Navy watch caps, but I could be wrong. It has been 56 years and my memory is hazy about some unimportant things. We dressed and were issued a hand towel, bathrobe, slippers, soap, comb, toothbrush, and tooth powder. Also, a book of rules and regulations. Then they took new mug shots and we were given our numbers. My number was 1118AZ. It still is!

Then the warden came in, Warden Swope, and we were given a lecture on what we could and couldn't do. There were more couldn'ts than could's. This included where to stand in the cell for head counts, that we got two showers a week, with clean clothes, we got a shave twice a week and learned what to do with the razors. If the blade was missing we were in trouble. Also: a haircut once a month, yard privileges and some kind of work if we obeyed the rules. We could also earn good time for working, plus a small wage, although there was no canteen to spend the money. Also we were told that if we tried to escape, we could be shot, and if we were caught escaping, we would spend years in segregation.

Then we were ready to go to our cells. We were taken up one at a time. I was the first one to go up to the cell house. The guard led me out of the shower room and up a flight of stairs to the cell house. My first impression of the cell house was how small it was. The length couldn't have been over 100 yards long and about 60 yards wide. There was a solid wall on the right side with one solid steel door and a wall with high barred windows on the left. There were only three tiers and two cell blocks. San Quentin across the bay had four cell blocks, was five tiers high and housed 3000 prisoners. There were about 300 prisoners in Alcatraz. There was about 15 feet separating the cell blocks, B-block on my left and C-block on my right, with cells facing each other in the center corridor. I later learned this corridor between the cell blocks was called 'Broadway.' The concrete floor was highly polished and everything else looked well cared for.

The guard took me to the third cell on Broadway. (#105, C-block) and another guard opened the cell door, which slid back. I was told to get in and then the door slammed shut with a sound I had never heard in any other prison. Most cell doors swung open and had to be locked with a key, but these doors were specially operated, so the mechanism held the cell doors tightly shut. The noise was much worse when all the cell doors of a tier were closed at the same time. It had the sound of doom and finality.

I put the few items I had been given on the shelves and looked around at a very small 5 by 9 cell. There was a steel bed, a thin mattress, two blankets, sheets, a pillow and pillow case, a small folding table, a small sink, with one tap, and a toilet with no seat. I stood up to the bars and listened to the cell doors close as the other prisoners I had arrived with were locked in their cells. There were a few prisoners in the cells across from me. They looked at me and I looked back at them. No one spoke, as there was nothing to say, and we had been told that loud talking was not permitted. Then I could hear the guards leaving the cell house and steel door closing behind them. In a few minutes the cell house was eerily quiet. The small cell and the loud sound of the doors closing was very depressing. I felt like I had been entombed. I was exhausted from the trip, and lay down on the bed and in a few minutes was asleep.

I woke up to the sound of cell doors opening, and then the sound of feet on metal stairs and concrete. The cons were coming in from work and soon, for the first time, I heard all the cell doors close at the same time. It shook the cell house! And me! Then someone hollered "count" and I stood up to the bars until the count was cleared. A matter of minutes. Then the same voice called out "lunch" and the doors opened and I followed the con from the cell on my left into the mess hall. A guard at the entrance directed me to one of two lines going to the serving tables. I did what the con in front of me did: picked up a tray, and helped myself to what I wanted. Then we moved to a table and when the table was full, about ten cons, five on each side, we all sat down and began eating. The mess hall was quiet because we were allowed to talk only in low voices. I don't remember what was served, but is was ok.

When we were all finished, we returned to the cell house and the cell doors slammed shut again. There was no loitering, smoking, or changing places in line allowed. The same thing happened again that afternoon. The only difference was that there always seemed to be a count, or the guards would just be checking up on us. I never knew which. So this is how the first day of many days, weeks, months, and years were going to be. It was a bleak future.

After three weeks of interviews and boredom, saved only by the books that I was given to read, I was informed that I would start to work the next morning in the kitchen. During the interviews I had said that I had wanted to work, and they knew I had worked in the mess hall in San Quentin. I didn't like working there, but in a few months I was transferred to the San Quentin hospital kitchen. We had much more freedom of movement there and stayed out of our cells longer.

So my work assignment was in the Alcatraz mess hall. Early the next morning my cell door opened and I went into the mess hall. My first cell was in the area where the kitchen cons cells were, so I didn't have to be moved. I hated working there from the first day and did sloppy work, but soon realized it wasn't fair to the other cons. We wore white clothes, got more showers, and more yard time. A month went by and although the kitchen crew got more yard time and more time out of their cells, I started to get angry and frustrated.

The cons in the kitchen felt this tension and stayed away from me. Soon I wasn't eating enough and sleeping very little. I paced my cell every night for hours. Three steps one way and then three steps back. I lost my interest in reading and my capability of escaping this existence by using my imagination to go anywhere I wanted for a little while. I asked for a work change and was told to stay where I was or stay in my cell and lose all privileges. I stewed about that for a few days, getting more mad and frustrated.

So I finally went to my answer for anything I didn't like. Violence! And it didn't matter whether it was a person or an object that I took my anger out on. Then late one night I broke up my cell. I tore the bed off the wall, and then the table. Then I used them to break up the sink and the toilet. Then I stuffed a towel down the toilet, flooding the cell floor and the cell house. If that wasn't enough, I tried to set fire to the mattress and everything else. But it just smoldered!

The cell house was in an uproar and I could hear shouts of "who blew their top?" The cons in the cells across from me, all three tiers, were egging me on, and I started to feel a little foolish as the madness left me because of the strenuous activity of getting rid of my frustrations. It was better this way than to take it out on some con who hadn't done anything to deserve a beating.

In about 15 minutes the Captain of the Guard, Bergen, showed up in front of my cell with three or four other guards. The cell door opened and Bergen told me to come out. My prison experience had taught me to never fight the guards. You absolutely could not win! So I came out.

8

We went around the corner of C-block and headed for a door in the West wall of the cell house. D-block.

D-block was a small block with 48 cells, 16 to a tier. All the cells were bigger than the cells in the main cell house. The two upper tiers were segregation, where some cons were kept for years. The main floor had ten regular cells and down on the far end was the 'hole.' Six cells with a barred front and a solid door outside that had a peep-hole in it. All six doors of these cells were open and we stopped in front of the middle one. I was told to strip and was throughly searched. Then Captain Bergen told me that I didn't need any clothes, because I had tried to burn everything, and to get into the cell. During all this time none of the guards had laid a hand on me. I entered a cell about 7 by 7 feet with nothing in it. There was a hole in one corner that I was told to defecate and urinate in, but not in those words. The flushing was controlled from out-side. The walls and the floor were steel. In a few minutes the doors closed. And then the light went out!

I had been in another dark hole several years earlier in the Los Angeles County Jail for beating another pris-oner very badly. I spent six weeks in that dark hole, but at least I had on long johns. And the jail had heat. The main cell house in Alcatraz has no heat, but there were radiators in D-block. Being naked, it wasn't long before I felt the cold, and knew that soon I would have to do something about it. So I started pacing, doing back and front push aways from the bars, pushups on the floor and squats. When I got tired I would lay down on my side, curled up in a fetal position and sleep until I woke up cold. And then do it all over again.

I was fed a big chunk of bread with water once a day and every three days, I had a meal consisting of a baked potato, a raw onion, some peas, all mixed up, and water. I didn't get scurvy, but I didn't gain any weight either! From the meal count I think I was in that dark strip cell for 29 days. I hadn't heard a voice and I did not make any sounds while I was in there. I have been told since then that a prisoner could not be kept in the dark hole more than 19 days. Also, for 14 days. But the rule makers in Alcatraz could do whatever they wanted. After all, they made the rules.

One morning both doors opened and I was told to come out. I was taken to a shower and after I dried off was given shorts, coveralls, and some slippers. Then I was moved up to the second tier to segregation. I was charged with inciting a riot and destroying government property, so I was going to be in segregation for a while.

This cell was bigger than those in the main cell house, about 7 by 12, had a steel bed with a mattress, and blankets, sheets, pillow, a writing table, a sink and a toilet. After that dark strip cell I felt like I had been moved to the St. Francis Hotel in San Francisco. In segregation we were fed three meals a day of regular prison food and had books to read. Also, we got a shower and shave once a week and a haircut once a month. I think we got to go to the yard for one hour a week. Of course, by ourselves. After getting acclimated to my new surroundings I lay down on the bed, covered up, got warm, and used my imagination which I had got back while I was in that dark hole, Then I went on a little trip. In a few minutes I fell into a deep sleep.

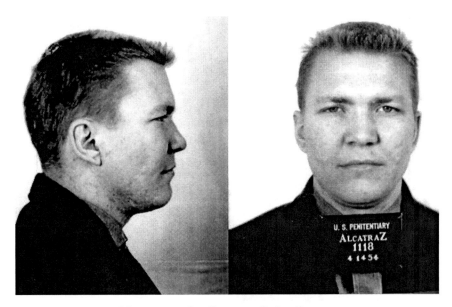

I knew now that I was really in Alcatraz.

The clothes fit and were well pressed.

The water was always hot. One of the problem spots on Alcatraz. The cons had to pay attention to what was going on around them.

Broadway. I can't believe this is all it is.

Same size as a pool table, 3 paces.

D-Block. "The Special Treatment Unit."

This was the deterrent used to insure the obedience of the rules.
The dark cells were the ultimate deterrent because no one
knew how they would react to being put in there.

Chapter Two
Alcatraz Rules
and Regulations

EVERY PRISON I WAS ever in had rules and regulations that the administrators needed to control the
population of prisoners. They always seemed to be very
stringent and unfair. Some of us had to be hit in the
head with a baseball bat to get the message that we
could no longer do what we wanted to do and when we
wanted to do it. But there were so many different types
of prisoners from every walk of life that there had to be
rules and regulations to fit every background. And the
way the prisoners interpreted the rules for themselves
sometimes depended on the crime they were convicted
of. Of course, the prisoners who thought they were innocent had a completely different view of the whole justice
system, and especially the unfairness of incarceration.
These 'innocents' complained loudly of every supposed,
or real, punishment meted out to them from the administration or the other prisoners.

Why from the other prisoners? And what kind of punishment was handed out from other prisoners? There's no way the prison population would put up with another prisoner's antics if they disturbed their ability to do their own time. Or if his actions caused the Warden to change the rules, and make doing time more difficult than it had been before. The cons punishment for this 'inmate' could be anything from a verbal lashing to a severe beating. And no one felt sorry for him. They only wished he would shut up!

From Juvenile Hall to Alcatraz, the rules were as different as day and night. And there were no 'gray' laws. They were black and white and left no doubt as to exactly what they said and how punishment was to be meted out. Every prisoner knew this, but it was still hard sometimes to not try to get around the rules. After all, we were human, even if most of the outside population didn't think so.

I broke the rules in every prison I was in, and sometimes even got away with it. Most of the rules I broke were minor, but some were very major. Like trying to escape, fighting, stabbing, or cussing out a guard or another prisoner. There were some prisoners who went after other prisoners sexually, but I think they were no different on the outside. If a man is inclined to that way of life, he will find a way and doesn't have to go to prison for enlightenment. Just because the prison gates close behind a man doesn't turn him into a homosexual. We all learn when we are young that a man's best friend is his right hand. Unless he is left handed!

In every prison I was in, one of the common rules was to keep yourself and your surroundings neat and clean. I think this was harder for prisoners in the juvenile justice system because they were used to their 'mommies' picking up after them and keeping their surroundings clean. What makes this even worse is that most, if not all juvenile living facilities, are in barracks. My brothers and I had to scrub floors, wash dishes, make our own beds, and learn every other type of household chore. Including how to cook. Home discipline. But learning these duties didn't make us any the less boys, later men, as we still fought among ourselves like any brothers do. So that part of prison was easy for me. My brothers and I also had our share of discipline, and learned the difference between right and wrong, and the consequences of not obeying the rules.

In later years when I was incarcerated in the Navy prison, San Quentin, Chino, McNeil Island, Leavenworth, and Alcatraz, all of these duties made doing time easier. Also, my four years in the U.S. Navy taught me to form a routine as soon as possible. Also to have everything kept in the same place all the time, which saved time and energy looking for something. This also helped me to OBEY THE RULES, and not be hassled by some infraction that I could avoid.

The first prison type environment I was in was Terminal Island Naval Prison in San Pedro, California. The guards were U.S. Marines who naturally thought that guarding prisoners was beneath them. Part of being a Marine is having pride, and what is prideful about guarding, and watching your back around a bunch of foul ups? The Marines, of course, acted to this situation naturally, as young men are want to do, and were uncivil and unnecessarily brutal when they had to use force to control some prisoners. The rules were more the Navy type rules, which means the military way of living was enforced. More spit and polish rules, rather than where you could go and when you could go there. Of course the crimes we were convicted of were much different than the crimes committed by the persons convicted and confined in state and federal prisons.

The Los Angeles County Jail was perhaps the worst lockup I was ever in. The prisoners were there waiting for trials, both in the state and federal courts. The jail was atop the Los Angeles Courthouse building, which was 15 stories tall. The top five floors were the jail. The prisoners were kept in 'tanks' of about 40 cells, two prisoners to a cell, with one more prisoner sleeping on the floor outside the cell on a mattress. This jail was run by the Los Angeles County Sheriff's Department.

And every 'tank' was run by a prisoner who meted out cells, and with the help of three other prisoners served the food brought in on wheeled carts with tubs of food. This #1 prisoner was the closest thing that I ever saw to a 'con boss', and he also picked his own crew and they kept everyone in line. There was every type of criminal thrown together in these 'tanks', which meant there were a lot of fights, some stabbings, and any other activity that human beings could do to each other.

The worst part of being in this jail was not knowing what was going to happen to you. So it was a relief to finally get sentenced and to know where you were going. The few months, or years in some cases, spent in that jail was an experience that is soon not to be forgotten. What were the rules? There were no rules! Just survival.

San Quentin is a big prison. Four cell blocks, five tiers high, with a population of about 2,500. There are huge recreation yards, with baseball, football, basketball, and weights to work out on. I thought that there were too many rules in San Quentin. But I came to understand they were needed to keep the prisoners in line. But you could still move around the cell house, go to the mess hall with whomever you wanted to, and there were canteen privileges to buy tailor-made cigarettes, candy or other extra items. The only paying industry was the jute mill. I went to San Quentin in 1950 when I was 23 years old. Just another young tough guy. I had a few minor infractions which came to nothing and had two fights. Violence was my way of coping with any problem. But San Quentin did teach me about the rules of prison, and how to get around them. And how to be a 'con' and not an inmate.

I was sent to the Federal Penitentiary on McNeil Island in Washington State after being found guilty of bank robbery. I was 26 years old. The rules there were similar to the rules at San Quentin. I didn't get along there very well and was recommended to be transferred to Alcatraz, but instead, I was sent to Leavenworth Federal Prison in Kansas.

The rules in Leavenworth were the same as the other prisons I had been in. Freedom of movement, lots of work details to choose from, and canteen privileges. In the six months I was there, I beat up two prisoners and tried to escape, which is one rule that the prison administrators really frowned on.

I arrived in Alcatraz just before my 27th birthday, in 1954. I thought it would be just another prison as far as the rules were concerned. Before the first day was over, I learned how very wrong I had been to think Alcatraz was just another prison. One of the first things I received was a rule book, which I was told to read and to keep it in my cell at all times. It was the 'INSTITUTION RULES & REGULATIONS.' This rule book had been in effect for 20 years and had been somewhat modified by Warden Swope in 1948 and Warden Madigan in 1956. The main rule deleted was the rule of silence, which was impossible to enforce.

There were 53 rules to be obeyed in Alcatraz, and before the first rule there was a written statement that said, "This booklet is issued for the information and guidance of inmates of the U.S. Penitentiary, Alcatraz, California. It outlines the institutions' routines and explains what is expected of you in the matter of conduct and work. You are expected to learn and obey the rules and to perform your assigned work to the best of your ability".

1. GOOD CONDUCT means conducting yourself in a quiet and orderly manner, and keeping your cell neat, clean and free from contraband. It means obeying the rules of the institution and displaying a cooperative attitude. It also means obeying the orders of Officials, Officers and other employees without delay or argument.

I am not going to quote every rule of Alcatraz here, but just say that the start of the rule book really got my attention. Morning wake up was the same every day and we got 20 minutes to wash up, make up the bed, and make sure the cell was in order. Every item in the cell had to be in a certain place. (See the cell set up diagram and the list of allowed items). Then after the first count we went to breakfast. One tier at a time, no talking, smoking, or changing places in line. We were moved to one of two lines in the mess hall by a guard. Picked up a tray and utensils and served ourselves the food. We took what we wanted, but had to eat all that we took. There was no moving around or loud talk, and when we were finished we returned directly to our cells. Roaming around the cell house was not permitted and neither was loitering on the galleries. Then another count. This routine happened every day at exactly the same time and was only broken by going to work or taking a shower.

There was no canteen in Alcatraz. Everything we had was furnished, and there was nothing extra without the specific permission from the Warden. There were no beards or mustaches allowed and we got a short haircut every month. We were issued two packs of tailor-made cigarettes a week, but there was a tobacco dispensary for roll your owns at the ends of the tiers. Also, matches. And only a certain amount of these items were allowed in the cell. Two nights a week a safety razor was placed on the bars of the cell and we had only a certain period of time to use them that night. Lock up and final count was at 4:30pm and lights out at 9:30pm.

Every aspect of a prisoner's life in Alcatraz was controlled. Including how many letters we could get a month and from whom, with one visit a month. Also, two times a month the privileged got to see a movie in the auditorium where they also held religious services on Sundays for those who wanted to go. I never attended either of these activities. I would rather stay in my cell and read. Or go to the yard. Going to the recreation yard was a privilege earned by staying out of trouble. We could go to the yard twice a day on Saturdays, Sundays, and holidays, if weather permitted. We moved from the cell house to the yard by tier, and we were not allowed to change position, smoke or talk at any time. When the yard period was over we lined up in the yard by tier and block and went through a metal detector before entering the cell house.

There were guards present in the recreation yard, which put them in jeopardy. There were also two guards at each end of the yard in towers, and they patrolled the yard around the top of the wall, which was about 20 feet high. They were armed with rifles and hand guns. They wouldn't hesitate to shoot, but that only happened twice while I was there. At any time a prisoner could be searched or pulled out of line and strip searched when going through the metal detector. There was absolutely no freedom of movement in the cell house, and we went directly into our cells. When all the prisoner were locked in their cells, there would be another count, and we had to again stand up to the bars of our cells until the count was cleared.

At first all of these rules and regulations really bothered me, but after my four months spent in D-block I became reconciled to the fact that I had to obey them. The administration would not allow the slightest deviation from the rules. All punishments were quick and final. Once I understood and accepted this as a fact, doing time in Alcatraz became easier. The regimentation and the monotony that came from it made the time spent in Alcatraz almost a blur, broken only by a fight, stabbing, riot, or other activity outside the normal routines.

Rule 53 GENERAL RULE; though not mentioned in these rules, any disorder, act, or neglect to the prejudice of good order and discipline, and any conduct which disturbs the orderly routine of the institution shall be taken cognizance by the Warden or his representative, according to the nature and degree of the offense, and punished at the discretion of the Warden or other authority.

This last rule underlines the harshness of 'doing time' in Alcatraz. It told us (the prisoners) that the administration, with the backing of all the guards, guns, steel bars, concrete, rules and the will to enforce them, could do whatever they wanted to do with the prisoners. So the last rule meant that the Warden not only enforced the written rules, but could interpret them in any way or make a new one to fit the act.

My one deliberate act at disobeying the rules, that I got caught for, happened soon after I arrived at Alcatraz, when I broke up my cell and set fire to everything in it.

I used the Alcatraz Rule Book to start the fire!

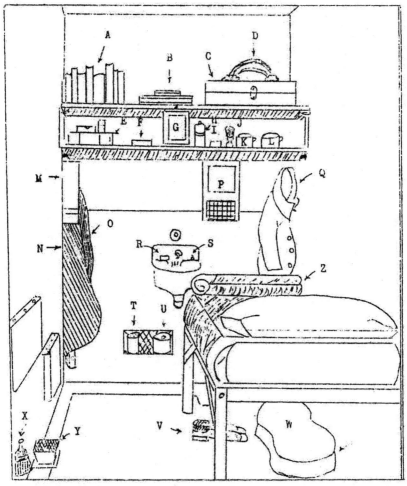

A - 12 Books(Maximum)	J - Shaving Brush	S - Sink Stopper
B - Personal Papers	K - Shaving Mug	T - Cleaning Powder
C - Paint Box etc.	L - Drinking Cup	U - Toilet Tissue
D - Radio Headphones	M - Face Towell	V - Extra Shoes & Slippers
E - Ash Tray & Tobacco	N - Bathrobe	W - Musical Instrument/Case
F - Extra Soap	O - Raincoat	X - Broom
G - Mirror	P - Calendar	Y - Trash Basket
H - Toothpowder	Q - Coat & Cap	Z - Extra Blankets
I - Razor & Blades	R - Soap	

N.B. Extra Blanket is to be folded neatly at foot of bed. Pillow at the head of
the bed toward the bars. Blankets are to be tucked in under the mattress.
Shoes, slippers and musical instruments & cases are to be under the bed with the
shoes or slippers under the leading edge of the bed.

Chapter Three
History

I WAS BORN MAY 22, 1927 in Provo, Utah. My family were all Mormons and I was raised in that faith. Two younger brothers were also born in Pravo. In 1933 one bed, some furniture, clothes in boxes and all of us were loaded into a flatbed truck and we moved to Lovell, Wyoming. This town was next to the Big Horn River and 12 miles south of Montana. My mother's family all lived there. Three brothers and two sisters. My father got a job as a carpenter. My grandparents had a big farm a few miles north of town and they fed a lot of people during the Depression. We lived there until 1937, and what I remember most was the spring the bluebirds got caught in a late blizzard. The snow turned blue with dead birds. I also learned to swim in a canal near our house.

We followed my father to Los Angeles, California in 1937, where his brother got him a job in a movie studio as a carpenter. We lived in Inglewood and moved to North Hollywood in 1938. I went to school, which was always easy for me. World War II started when I was 14 and by then, like most 14 year old kids, I thought I knew everything. One thing that I came to a certain conclusion is that a lot of Mormons were hypocrites, and so were a lot of people who professed to be religious and live by the tenets of their church. Only one person was pure, and He was crucified. The rest of us are only human and make mistakes.

In 1942, my parents divorced, and my mother, youngest brother Michael—who had been born in California and was only a year old, and I moved to Ogden, Utah. My father and brothers Darwin and Dean moved with my father to Provo, Utah. My mother got a job working nights in the train depot as a waitress and I started the 10th grade. That way one of us could take care of my brother. That was when my mother told me that R. V. Luke was not my father. A lot of things suddenly fell into place and on that day I became mean spirited and didn't care what happened to me or where I went.

After two months, when I learned there was a lot of money to be made working at a US Air Force Base just outside of Ogden, I quit school. I was paid for six weeks while I was trained in repairing aircraft engine carburetors. To a 15 year old, the money was great.

I became friends with a boy who worked there from St Louis, and one day shortly after we met he wanted to go home and join the Marines. St. Louis sounded good to me so we hopped on a bus and off we went. Soonafter we arrived he joined the Marines. In the meantime I got a job in East St. Louis, Illinois in the stockyards, even though I was only 15. But no one really cared as help was getting hard to find.

I worked on the cattle and horses unloading dock on the swing shift, 4 to 12. There were five of us, two older men in their fifties, and two in their middle twenties. And me, the kid. The two younger guys had just been released from prison and that was all they talked about. To me their conversation sounded like you could steal what you wanted and IF you got caught, then you had to do a little easy time.

Soon one of the guys told me that every night after work he prowled hotels looking for unlocked doors and he needed a lookout. I agreed a little too fast, as it sounded exciting. Every night after work we prowled the hotels and the money seemed great to me. Then I tried going into some of the rooms and found the stealing to be really simple. People sleep so soundly. We did this for two months.

One night I had to work overtime unloading hogs on the other side of the stockyard. No one liked that job. The hogs were in double decker railroad cars and they were big and mean. We had to go into the car and drive them out with a hog strap, made out of their own skin. If you weren't careful, they would run over you.

The next night Don didn't show up for work. A few nights later the police showed up looking for his partner. They seemed sure it was me and I had about 600 dollars in my pocket. But I was working! They took me to the station. I did not cooperate with them and soon convinced them that I was only 15 years old. They wanted to know where I wanted to go and in a few hours took me to the bus station and I bought a ticket to Los Angeles. As I boarded the bus the two detectives told me to stay out of St. Louis. I have never been back.

The bus station in Los Angeles was one block off Main Street. Skid row. I got a room in a cheap hotel, and in a few days became acquainted with another 16 year kid from Salt Lake City, Utah. He showed me a ring of master keys and skeleton keys. But said he didn't know what to do with them. I did, and we started going into apartment houses. There was no security, probably because of the war. We would knock on the doors and if no one answered we would use one of the keys to gain entry. Whatever we stole we took down to a flea market. This went on for about three months and sometimes we would go into three or four apartments a day. The day finally came when we turned our loot over to our guy in the flea market, and the police were suddenly there, and they had us!

After questioning me and getting no cooperation, the police left me in juvenile hall. Soon I was taken to juvenile court where I was astonished to hear this kid plead guilty to 132 counts of second degree burglary! I plead not guilty to the one count that we were picked up for. The kid's parents were there and the judge sentenced him to out of state probation in their custody. And they left! The judge told me that because I had not been cooperative he was sentencing me to six months in juvenile hall and three years probation.

I was sent to a forestry road camp and they had smokers (fights) every Saturday night. I was there about two weeks and challenged the champion after I had seen him fight. He didn't have a chance and only lasted about two minutes. Four days later three of his friends came up to me while we were working on the road and without a word started kicking me with their work boots. I went down and the pain made me do wild. As it always does. I was working with a short handled shovel and came up off the ground swinging. We all went to the hospital. One of them had a fractured skull and the other two had broken arms. I had to have a hernia operation and had a few other bruised on my head and body. I don't know where they were taken, but I was sent to the general hospital in Los Angeles.

My mother had moved back to Los Angeles and after five weeks in the hospital I went and stayed with her and my little brother. I turned 17 and as soon as I could, I joined the Navy. Boot camp was in San Diego, California.

I spent six weeks in Gulfport, Mississippi in engineering school and was transferred to Treasure Island in San Francisco Bay, the Embarkation holding barracks. Everyone there had liberty 24 hours a day. About ten days later I was ferried over to Alameda to my first ship, the APA 149 Audabon, a troop transport ship. We stopped in Hawaii for a few days and only the crew got liberty. Then we sailed for the South Pacific. We carried the 110th Seabee Battalion and went to Samar Island in the Philippines. While the Seabees were being off loaded, I was informed that I had been transferred to the 110th Seabees!

That didn't set well with me so I made a nuisance of myself by going into the jungle looking for snipers. I had been issued a rifle. The only thing I shot were trees and coconuts. Three weeks later I was called into the Executive Officer's office, which was on the second floor of a building on the waterfront. He took me over to the window overlooking the harbor and pointed to a tanker and said, "That's your new ship." It was a fleet tanker, the USS Taluga AO62. It carried 500,000 gallons of aviation gasoline and oil. I was on that ship for two and a half years. Several months later the war ended and we were with the first U.S. ships to enter Tokyo Bay, Japan. We had liberty every other day in Yokosuka, Yokohama and took the train to Tokyo. On the train to Tokyo we went through Kamakura and Little Kamakura cities, where the giant gold plated Buddha stood. It was about 50 feet high, in a sitting position. I have never forgotten that astonishing sight.

My ship sailed on December 20, 1945 and two days later we arrived in Seoul, (Inchon) Korea. We were there for Christmas and I still think it is the coldest place in the world. We then headed east across the north Pacific Ocean and several days later entered San Francisco Bay. The ship passed Alcatraz and stopped in Martinez long enough to get all the cargo fuel tanks steamed cleaned. We then proceeded to Vallejo, where we stayed for about a month to get some repairs done. Vallejo was a good liberty town.

My ship left San Francisco Bay in early February 1946 and I began a two year adventure that every boy dreams of. Perhaps every young person has a dream of sailing around the world and seeing exotic places. Understand that this tanker's cruising speed was about 20 knots, 25 miles an hour, so we spent a lot of days seeing nothing but water!

Our first stop was in Honolulu, Hawaii for a few days of liberty and the next stop was Hong Kong, China for a few more days of liberty. Hong Kong was very impressive. Then we sailed south and then west through the Strait of Malacca, a seemingly narrow passage. We next stopped at Columbo, Ceylon, (Sri Lanka) for a few days. I remember the two big tug boats that helped the ship into the man-made harbor. They were named the Samson and Hercules. The British had been in Ceylon for over 100 years and the architecture was part English and part Indian. My buddy Ivan and I made a trip to Kandy, in the northern mountains to see the jewel mines. The mines had huge entrances and had been mined for centuries. We were fortunate to see a spectacle on one of our trips to Kandy, of a King Cobra religious ceremony. One of the priestesses coaxed a 12 foot snake out of one of the closed mines, danced in front of it and kissed it on the head! What could be more exiting than to see that? Alcatraz for the first time?

We then proceeded west in the Indian Ocean and then northeast into the Persian Gulf. We stopped in either Ras at Tanura or Bahrain in Saudi Arabia. Our ship was tied up to a long dock, about half a mile long, with several large pipes along the top. It took three or four days to fill the tanker, as we carried over 500,000 gallons of oil. It was cold there in the winter and very hot in the summer. Liberty was the long walk to the American refinery and oil field workers' recreation area, which consisted of a theater, bowling alley, pool room, and bar. And it was all air conditioned! There was nothing else in the whole region that was interesting to a sailor. Unless you liked sand! We made eight trips into the Gulf and couldn't leave fast enough.

Our first trip from the Gulf was through the Red Sea and into the Suez Canal where we anchored in the Big and Little Lakes to wait for the tide to change, so all the ships that were waiting could go against the tide and be able to have steerage. The tide lasted about six hours. Coming back from Suez on the north side of the canal we did the same thing. Waited for the tide. There was nothing to see going through the Suez Canal but the high banks of sand. From the bridge we could see over the banks and could see even more sand.

We sailed west to the Mediterranean and next stopped in Tangiers, North Africa. Tangiers was the most beautiful city I ever saw. The city rose from the sea up to the top of the mountain behind it. All the buildings were white and shining in the sun. You could see Tangiers for miles out to sea before you arrived there. It was an open port, as was Casablanca, which meant there was no tariff on any goods bought there. Liberty was great! A sailors paradise. I bought several bottles of Chanel #5 and White Shoulders perfume for five bucks a bottle and gave them out for months to some of the girls I met.

We then headed past Gibralter and into the Atlantic Ocean. It seemed like a long trip to Key West, Florida for a short four day stop and then on to Norfolk, Virginia. Ship City. We were in Norfolk about two weeks. There were a lot of sailors, marines and liquor. It seemed like every night we got into some kind of fight with either sailors or marines, or both. That was called liberty!

We left Norfolk and headed back the way we had come, with another stop in Tangiers. Then Suez City, where we stayed for four days waiting for our turn to get through the canal. My buddy Ivan and I had the chance to take a train 40 miles to Cairo, Egypt. We went to the Casbah, which was the only place a sailor could get what he needed or wanted. We made one more trip like that sometime during the next year.

After the ship was loaded with oil again, our next stop was Manila, in the Philippines. We always stayed in Manila for two or three weeks. Great liberty! Then we proceeded North in the China Sea to the Yangzte River, in China, which had a mouth so wide that we could not tell when we actually entered the river. After about 20 miles we turned north into the Wangpoo River and up to Shanghai, China. The amount of people on the streets and in sampans on the river, day and night, was astonishing. I volunteered to go through the initiation of the Wangpoo River Rats, which was run by a bunch of Asiatic Navy Chiefs. I pulled a rickshaw, ate rice and drank Shanghai scotch for three days. It almost killed me. It was almost as bad as the dark hole in Alcatraz. That initiation made the Crossing of the Equator initiation look like a walk in the park.

My buddy Ivan's family came from Russia and when the revolution took place in 1917 they came to America and became citizens. Russia became Red, the Soviet Union. And all those who left the county became White Russians. There was a big colony of them in Shanghai and Ivan naturally gravitated to them, and I went with him. He spoke fluent Russian. We had a great time with them during the three or four weeks the ship was there. When we left Shanghai and headed back to Manila and on to the Persian Gulf again, Ivan stayed behind in

Shanghai. I never saw or heard from him again and wondered many times since then what happened to him after the communists took over China in 1949.

The ship made several more trips to the Persian Gulf for oil, one more time to Norfolk, Virginia. And we alternated stops between Singapore and Columbo on each trip. Singapore was good liberty.

In early 1948 we again sailed across the Pacific, east this time, and entered the Puget Sound in Washington State. We went to the Navy Shipyard in Bremerton and were put into dry dock for bottom scraping, painting, and some refitting. We were there for three months. My minority hitch was almost up as I was approaching 21 and I decided to ship over and stay in the Navy. I asked, and assumed, that I would be assigned to another ship or shore duty. But that was not to be. After I came back from a short leave I was informed that I was to stay on the USS Taluga AO62 until it was decommissioned. No one knew when that would be.

For the first time in years I became depressed and angry. One night I went on liberty and just kept on going south, even though I had more leave coming. I visited my brothers in Los Angeles. They all had moved back there during the war. My mother had remarried a Master Sargent in the Army and they were living in Lawton, Oklahoma, where he was stationed at Fort Sill. So I went and stayed with them for a month. After 62 days of being AWOL I turned myself in, thinking I would simply be discharged, and given an Honorable Discharge.

But the Navy didn't think it that way and I was given a General Court Martial, which was held on

Yerba Buena Island in San Francisco Bay. I was found guilty of going AWOL and sentenced to one year in Navy prison. The sentence was suspended and I was sent to a retraining barracks in Vallejo. I wasn't to get out of the Navy after all!

When I got to the Mare Island Naval Shipyard in Vallejo, I was in a terrible mood, had a chip on my shoulder, and was spoiling for a fight. There were Marine guards there and one of the Sergeants and I immediately started butting heads. This went on for about a month until I had enough and I went after him and beat him up really bad. The other Marines naturally roughed me up a little, and then put me in a wooden stockade inside a room under guard at all times. I was let out to eat regular meals, wash and go to the head, and then back into the box. There were two holes about waist high in the door, big enough to put my hands through. After I entered the box, the door was closed. I had to put my hands through the holes in the door and they were handcuffed. About a week later I was taken out and transported by van to the Terminal Island Naval Prison in San Pedro, California. The trip took about eight hours.

In the Navy prison all the prisoners lived in dormitories and slept in three-tiered bunk beds. There were very few cells. I came in there with a chip on my shoulder and looking for a fight. It didn't take long before some one challenged me. And it took me only a few seconds to put him on the floor. One of the Marine guards saw what had happened and we were immediately taken to another building. I had found out where the cells were. Not only cells, but some unusual punishment holes. A door four feet square, about three feet off the floor with a metal bar about a foot above the door. I was stripped to my shorts, searched, and got into the box, feet first, which was about seven feet deep. The solid door closed, it had a vent in it, and it was dark. If you had to go to the head, you knocked on the door until a Marine guard let you out. Then you went right back in that little hole that you couldn't even sit up in. We were fed bread and water for five days. On the sixth morning the door opened and I was let out. I went back to the dormitory, same bunk, took a shower, put on clean clothes, and went back to doing time. No one else challenged me.

A few days later another prisoner approached me and said he had witnessed the fight and knew I had been trained. He told me they had a boxing team there and fought in smokers every Saturday night, sometimes with outside fighters. So for the rest of my time in the Naval prison, I worked out on the heavy bag, sparred, ran around the yard and fought in smokers. I had several hundred dollars and could get the little things I wanted from the commissary.

Ten months later I walked out of the Naval prison. My brother Darwin was waiting for me and he took me to my mother's house, as she had moved back to California. I tried my hand at boxing on the outside and made a living as a gym boy, (punching bag). That only lasted a few months.

Then I was introduced to a guy who said he needed a driver to drive him around Los Angeles. He said he was a gambler and he did gamble a lot. But soon I found out that he was also casing the bookies and then later holding them up. Sounded like easy money to me. So if there was a bookie that knew him, I would do the job. I was traveling with a young women that had two kids, and we moved from motel to motel so we couldn't be placed in the same spot at any time. We knew the mob (Mickey Cohen) controlled the bookies, and they frowned on any one stealing their money.

One morning we were on our way to a job, and I was driving the stolen car. There were two pistols in the glove box. Suddenly there were flashing lights behind us and my partner told me he couldn't handle any kind of shootout, which really hadn't entered my mind.

There was some kind of problem with the license plate. It's always the little things that get you caught. They found the guns, pulled their own guns' and we were placed under arrest. This happened in Long Beach, California, a suburb of Los Angeles, and a few days later we were transported to the Los Angeles County Jail. I was picked out of a lineup and charged with 1st degree armed robbery. I plead guilty to car theft and carrying concealed weapons, and then testified that my partner and the girl knew nothing about the car or guns. He was found guilty and was sentenced to one to ten and one to five years and because of his extensive record in New York was sent to Folsom prison. The last time I saw him, he said, "take care" and I never saw him again. His name was Jacob Wessenfeld. The girl was found innocent and was released.

About a month later I was found NOT GUILTY of the armed robbery. I was sentenced to one to ten and one to five years to run concurrently. The sentence was then suspended and I was sentenced to three years probation with the first year in the county jail. I was moved up to the top floor of the county jail and made a trusty. The only job in that jail was in the kitchen, taking food down to the holding tanks. And that was my job. It was another dormitory style living condition. I made friends with two guys who had done time on the Texas chain gang, where one had cut one Achilles tendon so he wouldn't have to pick cotton.

Within a month, on a weekend, the assistance steward called me into his office and told me a prisoner named Joe Spinelli had told him that I was stealing sugar and pepper and selling them down in the tanks. If the regular steward had been there, I am sure he would never have used another prisoner's name.

I went back to the dormitory and told my buddies what had happened and they said Spinelli was out on the roof. We could go out there to get some sun and air, as there was a high wall around the perimeter. I went out on the roof and he was sitting on a bench with his head back, legs stretched out and sound asleep. I went up, braced my knees on each side of him, and hit him four times. He didn't make a sound. I walked back into the dorm, asked my buddies "how's that." They said great and then we went down to the dining room and had lunch.

Twenty minutes later several sheriff's deputies came into the mess hall and scattered out. One came up to me and asked if my name was Luke. I answered "yes" and he called the others over. After searching me, they told me to put my hands in my pockets, then grabbed my hands through my pants. A very effective was of immobilizing a person.

We went down one flight to the hospital and into a treatment room, where a doctor was working on Spinelli. He was a bloody mess, in shock and unconscious. They asked me if I had done that and I denied having anything to do with it, although I had seen several prisoners out on the roof when I took care of the rat. Not too far away from the hospital in another corridor was a small room with two solid doors in the wall. After I was strip searched, they gave me a pair of long johns and told me to get into one of the cells.

There was nothing in that cell but a toilet without a seat. The door closed and the light went out. At least it wasn't as bad as that box in the Naval prison. I was fed bread and water and every three days a full meal, I can't remember what it was. They gave me a mattress and blanket every night and took them away in the morning. I immediately started pacing and working out.

Six weeks later the door opened. They took me to a shower, gave me some clean jail clothes, and gave me my shoes back. I was moved down to the back of a holding tank where the Mexican drug users were kept. I was locked in a cell and left there for three weeks. When they brought the food cart in, a sheriff's deputy would come back with the trusty, open the separating gate, and I would be fed, after everyone else got what they wanted. I was there for three weeks, and then was moved to a regular holding tank, after getting a shower and more clean clothes.

The #1 in the holding tank I was put in, named Wayne, asked me where the hell I had been. A lot of the prisoners in that tank had heard of what I had done. I had lost about 15 pounds, as the diet I had been on was not conducive to looking well fed. The jail was overcrowded and there were two to a cell, with one sleeping on the floor outside. The cell doors were never locked. Wayne immediately told the guy who had the lower bunk in the second cell to move his mattress out into the corridor. I really appreciated that and we became friends.

I was taken back to court and the judge told me he was sending me to a place where I could get some help. That was nice of him. The judge then proceeded to violate my probation and sent me to San Quentin for the term prescribed by law. At least I knew what was going to happen to me and I would get out of the Los Angeles County Jail!

Wayne had been sentenced to five years to life for armed robbery and a few weeks later we were on the same chain to San Quentin, on the San Francisco Bay. I arrived at San Quentin in May 1950 and was given #A14899. My first cell was in the north block, the fish tank, and I was there for six weeks, for interviews and orientation. I was assigned to the main line kitchen and worked mostly on the main serving line.

There was one riot in the mess hall while I worked there. A dispute about tops or bottoms. All the tables faced one way, with an aisle about two feet wide between. After a prisoner went through the line, if he didn't like what was being served, he could get all the bread he wanted. After he sat down a con would come down the aisle with a stainless steel bucket with kidney beans, and ask "tops or bottoms? Which meant mostly beans or mostly soup. The fight, and then the riot, broke out when the con didn't like what he got and the server dumped the bucket of hot beans on his head. Then trays, food, and everything else started flying. If somebody had a grudge, he would go looking for that con. After a few shots were fired from the gun rail, about 30 feet off the floor, every one quieted down and went back to their cells. Sometimes it didn't take much to get all the cons riled up. In two months I was transferred to the hospital kitchen, which was a good job.

There weren't many jobs in San Quentin. The main one was the jute mill, where jute was made for gunny sacks, rope, and other grass products. The cons earned a little money there to spend in the canteen. I had plenty of money and didn't need to work in the jute mill. Thank you very much. After I left San Quentin, some one finally burned it down, after many attempts.

I was in San Quentin about 20 months and then was transferred to Chino in southern California. Chino was a medium security prison and we lived in barracks. I played some football and didn't work as I was a short timer. A con I knew, who was a junkie (dope addict) asked the catholic priest if he could start a singing group. He was a musician and got permission. He ended up with two tenors, two baritones, and a basso. I was one of the baritones! We practiced religious hymns.

On Easter Sunday in 1952 the priest held a sunrise service and about 500 prisoners and their families were there. We, the choir, sang Ave Marie, and every one said it was very good. They recorded the proceedings that day and I have often wondered if that recording was still around somewhere.

I was released from Chino May 12, 1952, and took a bus to Los Angeles. My brother Darwin got me a job in an egg plant, since you couldn't get released on parole unless you had a job. I worked in the warehouse loading trucks with crates of eggs. The egg plant was across the street from Universal movie studios and I lived in the small Universal Hotel next door.

In a few months I started going with a young lady who worked with me. She had a little girl and soon I was going over to her parents' house for dinner. She had a brother about 20 years old who had one of the best tenor voices I had ever heard.

One evening I was contacted by an old girlfriend who told me some guy wanted to meet me. So I went over to her house and met a guy named Joseph Dellamure from Brooklyn. We talked for a while and then he told me he had been looking for a bank to rob, and that he had found one that seemed suitable. I was interested as I hadn't learned my lesson yet. We went down to Los Angeles a few days later and looked at an old Bank of America that had small bars on a back window. The bank was on a corner with a bus stop in front. That posed no problem because the blinds were closed every night and only opened just before the bank opened the next morning.

About four o'clock one morning we parked a car around the corner from the bank. Joe and I were in the back seat and his girlfriend and her sister were in the front. They dropped us off and were to return later to pick us up. We went into the alley and in a few minutes we had spread the bars, opened the window that was not locked, and went inside. We waited in a room with the door cracked open until we saw that all the employees were in the bank and then we came out with hoods on and took control. Joe was armed with a German Schmeisser machine gun, (burp gun), and I had a pistol. We put the employees, four women and one man, into the room we had hidden in.

There was only one problem. The first employee to enter the bank that morning had opened the blinds! We were wearing hoods, so I took mine off and calmly walked to the front of the bank and closed the blinds. There were several people waiting for the bus, but none seemed to pay any attention to what was going on inside the bank. The vault had already been opened and it didn't take us long to empty that and the cashiers' cash boxes. Then we moved the employees to the vault and closed the door, but didn't lock it. Joe put the burp gun in the valise with the money and we walked out of the front door, around the corner to the car, and drove off.

We arrived back where Joe was staying, very pleased with ourselves, and split the money. It was a very nice haul! We then said our goodbyes and I went home and found a place to hide my share of the loot. And went on with my life as if nothing had happened. Except all of a sudden I had enough money to buy a car and a few other things.

Three weeks later I was sitting in an ice cream parlor with my girl friend, her mother, and little girl, when about a dozen men, FBI and police, came in with drawn guns, walked right over to me and arrested me. The women were scared but were not bothered in any way.

Several days later I was in a federal court room with my attorney, who I had used several years earlier in an armed robbery trial. My attorney had told me that Joe and his girlfriend had been arrested in New Orleans a day earlier. He still had the machine gun, and his share of the loot and he had left the Bank of America wrappers on the money! They were arrested and his girlfriend told the police who I was and where to find me and her sister, who was in Miami. Joe plead guilty to bank robbery and I plead not guilty. My attorney told me a few weeks later that Joe had served time in both Sing Sing and Dannemora prisons in New York for armed robbery. He was sentenced to ten years in prison. His girlfriend and her sister plead guilty to accessory and were sentenced to 18 months in prison.

My first trial ended in a hung jury and after a second trial I was found guilty, even though they found no money from the bank or a gun. It seemed one of the employees from the bank made a positive identification of me through a small opening in the vault door. And especially my cold blue eyes, she said.

So I was sentenced to ten years in a federal penitentiary. We could have been given 25 years on each count, and Joe and I were soon on our way to McNeil Island on the Puget Sound in Washington State. Very near Bremerton Naval Base. Where had I heard that name before?

McNeil Island was a larger island than Alcatraz and in my opinion would have been much more difficult to escape from. The Puget Sound was a lot bigger than San Francisco Bay and the currents more treacherous. But I was not there long enough to find this out, as I had a disciplinary problem within two months, (fighting and an escape risk), and was transferred to Leavenworth Federal Penitentiary in Kansas.

The trip to Leavenworth, in a prison bus, took two days and we spent one night in an old city Jail in Salt Lake City, Utah. The cells were rusty, dirty, and cold, with a solid steel door and must have been built in the previous century. On top of that, the food was so bad it was almost inedible. I was glad to leave there!

We arrived in Leavenworth in the evening and after being searched, showered, clothed, and given a new mug shot, I was put in a big cell with five other prisoners. Another fish tank. There had been about ten of us on the bus, and two of them were put in the same cell. The others were being transferred to Atlanta, Louisburg, the Springfield Medical facility or other federal prisons. Including my partner, Dellamure.

I was in that cell for about a month and only went out for showers twice a week, and to the mess hall to eat. We did get books, canteen privileges, and some magazines to read. And of course with six men in the same cell, there were a lot of stories to tell. We had no trouble with each other and the month passed OK. My next cell was on the top tier of A-block and it was a two man cell.

Soon I made friends with three cons who hung out together and they accepted me, after they found out they could trust me. Of course there are no secrets in prison, everyone knows everything they want to know about another con. And your reputation goes with you. I can only remember one of them. His name was Milton (Slats) Winchell, #69863. He was a tall rawboned guy about five years older than me. The movies always show a lot of gangs, and it is usually cons with the same interests. So I guess we were a gang. And the movies always show some big con boss running the prison. With two or 3000 alpha males around, I don't think he would last very long. I never saw a con boss. Besides the prison authorities—in order to maintain control—would bury him so deep, they would have to pump sunlight down to him!

I had one problem soon after with another con. I was coming through a narrow corridor between the cell house and the yard, when I met another con coming the other way. He deliberately shouldered me and said "watch where you're going, punk." In about ten seconds he was on the floor begging me to stop kicking him, which I was doing, after I had knocked him down. I told him to be careful what he said after that, and walked off. I never had any trouble after that. The word gets around, and if somebody asks for trouble, they can always find more than they can handle. Including me!

One day Slats told me he had a plan to escape, but it would take two guys. Of course I was interested. I had just started a ten year sentence. I will relate now what happened about a month later.

This was on January 18, 1954 and it got dark about 4:30pm, especially when it was cloudy. That was dinner time, when the cell house emptied and went to the mess hall. They all went east and since it wasn't unusual for some cons to leave a few minutes later, no one paid any attention to us. As soon as the last con had passed, we left our cells and headed west and down the stairs on the west end of the cell house. We had our blankets to throw over the ten foot barbed wire on top of the fence outside the cell house. Also a bar spreader that another con had made us. The window embrasures were about ten feet off the floor and I boosted Slats up, handed him the blankets and bar spreader, then he pulled me up. We thought we had about 15 minutes to spread the bars before the guards came around that end of the cell house as they checked the cells for any stragglers. Once we had the bars spread, we would be over the fence and gone. Of course we didn't know how much time we had before the next count was done after every one was back in their cells after dinner. There was a guard tower outside the fence on the corner, but we had seen from the second tier that when the guard shift changed at 4pm, the tower was abandoned for the night.

We had been taking turns working on the bars for about five minutes and were making good progress and in about five minutes more would be out the window and on the ground outside the cell house. Then someone, a guard, hollered "what's going on down there." The guard was on the top tier and was looking right down at us. Then he started blowing his whistle and hollering "escape." We came down out of the window and scattered, but it didn't take long before we were caught.

I was hustled over to isolation, stripped, and thoroughly searched. Then they put me in a large cell, dressed in coveralls and slippers. There was only a toilet in there and nothing else. Soon the door opened and they told me to come out and I was questioned by, I supposed, the warden. Then I was given a thin mattress and a blanket. The next morning they opened the door, took the mattress and blanket and gave me a large piece cut from a loaf of something that tasted like it was made from vegetables. Also some water. In the evening I was fed spaghetti, cooked in milk, and a raw onion. This went on for three weeks, with an occasional questioning session. During the second week I was in "the hole," and I started walking up and down, singing "we three are all alone, my echo, my shadow, and me," at the top of my lungs. It wasn't long before the peephole in the door was opened and I was told to shut up or they would come in and shut me up! I got the message. Then I was moved upstairs to another cell, with a bed, table, toilet, and sink, and had books to read. I was in there about a month.

Our escape attempt was on the 18th of January and on the 19th , two cons, William Ward, #69155 and Harold K. Hayes, #70371, grabbed two guards. They tied them up separately and got their keys. One gaurd got loose and sounded the alarm. After negotiations, the cons surrendered. One or both of them implicated Slats and me in their attempted escape, or whatever it was. I could never understand how that was possible, when we were already in isolation. They were never sent to Alcatraz. During my time in segregation I was taken before a good time board, and was told that one or both of the 'inmates' in the attempted escape on the 19th had said that both Winchell and I had been part of that escape attempt. They took all my good time that I had earned.

One morning about 4am the door opened and I was handcuffed and taken to another part of the prison. There was a prison train car there, bars on the windows and they were blacked out. They got me aboard and the first person I noticed was Slats, whom I hadn't seen since our escape attempt. We said hello and then I was shackled ankle to ankle to another prisoner, who I didn't know. I found out later some of the cons had come from Atlanta, and we all knew where we were going. Alcatraz!

When we were all secured, the guards left the car, but there were several Federal US Marshals in the car, separated from us by heavy screens. There was one toilet and we could use it after we got permission. Two cons at a time, of course. We heard a engine and felt a thud and soon started moving. About an hour later we were hooked up to another car. I found out later it was in Lawrence, Kansas. We started moving and I could tell by the light from a window in the back of the car that we were heading west.

In about two hours I figured that we weren't in Kansas any more, and we absolutely were not going to Oz!

4 months old. Everyone has to be a baby once.

David Nelson-7, Robert Luke-7, Darwin Luke-5,
Beverly Nelson-4, Dean Luke-2.

The Robertsons 1942 — Ray, John, Snell, LaPrele,
Beryl (mother) and Helen.

February 20, 1945 — Home on boot camp leave.
17 years old.

On liberty in Columbo, Ceylon. 19 years old.

1948—Last US Navy picture. 21 years old.

Probably what a mug shot should look like.

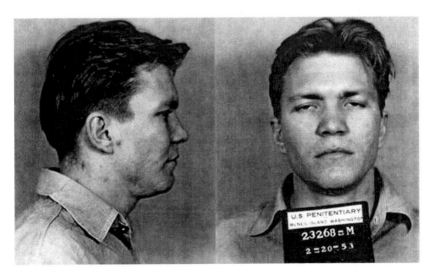

Recommended for transfer to Alcatraz for assault on another prisoner,
a bad attitude, and cussing a guard. Sent to Leavenworth instead.

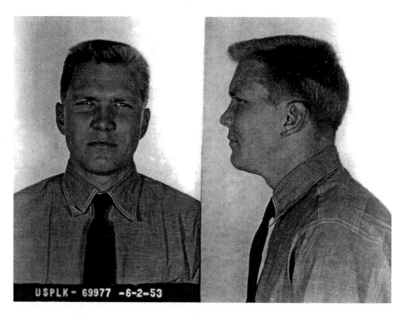

USPLK- 69977 -6-2-53

Not here long. Sent to Alcatraz for trying to escape.

Chapter Four
Epiphany

FOUR YEARS HAVE PASSED since I was released from 'D' block and segregation. My next cell was in B-block, third tier, the second cell. I was there for two years. Alvin (Creepy) Karpis was in the first cell. He ran with Ma Barker and her boys. To my recollection we never spoke or even acknowledged each other. Which was fine with me, as I was more or less a loner.

My next assignment was in the glove shop. Sitting at a sewing machine for hours every day was not my idea of doing easy time. So instead of breaking up my cell to get out of the glove shop, I just made lousy gloves. I was transferred to the laundry, where I stayed until my release about four years later. I still did a lot of reading and when we had yard time, I would walk, and play handball or baseball. Or just sit on the big steps and look over the wall, where I could see the northern part of San Francisco, the Golden Gate Bridge, Angel Island and parts of Marin County. This view didn't necessarily bother me, as it was just a nice view. And very different from the concrete, bars, and sullen faces of my fellow prisoners. The monotony and the regimentation of the prison routine turned time into a blur for me. Every day was the same. Get up, eat, shower, shave, have a haircut, have yard time, go to work, and lights out. Plus the 53 rules and regulations we had to be aware of.

I really believe that this same routine went on day after day, month, after month and year after year made doing time easier. To this day I am still very aware of time and still do the same things at the same time each day. Only certain things that happened to me stand out in my memory. There had been a few incidents in the last four years that are worth mentioning. The first was a stabbing in the yard. A con named Simcox had come out to the yard with a list of five names—cons he figured needed taking care of. The first con he saw was a in-mate named "Dog Mann" who was a known informer. Simcox stabbed him seven or eight times, assumed he was dead, dropped the shiv, and waited until the guards grabbed him and took him to D-block. "Dog" really did look dead. He was sure bloody! Then the guards took "Dog" by the heels and dragged him up the steps into the cell house. We could hear his head hitting every step on the way up. I heard later that after "Dog" was in the hospital for a while, he suddenly asked why his face was covered. He was alive! They took him to a hospital somewhere and in two months he was back. All the cons in the yard were taken back to their cells.

Simcox and another prisoner named Garvin were U.S. Army prisoners. They had been convicted of mutiny and other charges, and had gotten life sentences.

They could not be controlled in an army detention facility, so they were brought to Alcatraz. Simcox was a big, strong guy, a light heavyweight fighter, and the dominant one. Garvin was more slight and very quiet. I never knew exactly what their relationship was and really didn't care. Garvin had committed some breach of the rules and was in D-block, segregation. The word was that Simcox went after "Dog Mann" so he could be near Garvin.

Garvin was the first to get out of segregation and in several months Simcox was released back into the population. Shortly after that, Simcox killed Garvin down in the shower room. I don't know if Simcox was tried for killing Garvin, but he was still in segregation when I left Alcatraz.

Two other incidents were related and happened about a year apart. Both were started by the same con. The first started in the mess hall, when the con got up from the table and without a word, turned the table over! That action was catching, and in a minute all the other tables were turned over. The instigator was hustled out of the mess hall and over to D-block. The rest of us were searched for any cutlery, and moved back to our cells. This happened at the noon meal and we stayed in our cells until the next morning, when we went in to breakfast. The mess hall looked like nothing had happened, but it must have been as real mess. No wonder I didn't want to work in the mess hall!

The second incident with the same con happened in the yard. He was playing dominoes or bridge and suddenly turned over one of the heavy tables, and broke off one of the two by four legs. A few other cons did the same, and headed for the other corner of the north end of the yard. Home plate for the baseball field was in the middle, with the wall at that end of the yard used as the back stop. He went after the Negroes, who used that corner for their games. There were only seven or eight of them in Alcatraz and they were his target. Of course, they immediately retaliated, broke off the legs of their tables, and a small riot started. A few other fights broke out in the yard, as there are always arguments or differences to be settled.

The guards up on the wall blew their whistles a few times and then fired two or three shots into the air. The melee stopped and the instigator was taken away to D-block. Again. I think that every once in a while he just needed something different. Like a little trip to isolation. There were a few bruises and bumps, but no one was badly hurt. I was at the other end of the yard playing handball and didn't get involved. At that time I didn't have anything to settle with any con, and I guess none had any issues to settle with me.

The next incident did involve me, and although I knew at the time that it could send me to the hole and segregation again, I couldn't seem to avoid the confrontation. I was working in the laundry, where we did the laundry for the prison and some of the military bases near Alcatraz. There were six dryers and they were as big as a Volkswagon Bug. Just to the north of them were two rows of industrial washers, six to a row. The sheets and other items were brought over in laundry carts to the dryers, where I and another con, Harvey Carrignan,

#935AZ, loaded and unloaded them from the dryers. It really was a two man job, but this guy liked to hang out in the dry cleaning room, where two of my friends worked. One friend was 'Slats' Winchell, who I had tried to escape from Leavenworth with and the other was a con nicknamed 'Dago', who was an ex-fighter.

'Dago', myself and two other pugs would, during breaks, go to the end of the laundry in an open space and shadow box. It was good exercise. This guy I worked with on the dryers wanted to be part of our group, but he came on too quick, and we didn't trust him. We also knew that he had a 'shiv' stashed somewhere in the laundry and always had it on his person. He was also a convicted killer.

One day when I had had enough of Carrignan's crap, and no longer caring about the consequences, I went looking for him. He was in the dry cleaning room, which had a heavy screen around it. There were no hidden nooks or any other places to get out of sight of the guards. Knowing he had a 'shiv', I simply walked up to him and hit him with my fists four or five times. He went down unconscious and I turned and went back to work on the dryers. Someone called the guards and he told them he had slipped and fallen down. Except his jaw was shattered and so were his cheekbones. No telling who else had seen this happen, but the next morning I was kept in my cell. Later I was taken in front of the disciplinary board and asked if I knew anything about the incident, and they looked closely at my hands for bruises or cuts. I told them that all I knew was what I had heard, but they didn't believe me. Since there was no forth coming evidence I was told to go back to work. I never saw this con again. He was transferred that day to Springfield Medical Facility in Missouri. Perhaps I had done him a favor to get him out of Alcatraz!

In 1957 or '58, the door to the laundry opened and in walked five men. One I recognized immediately, I don't know how, as Bill Russell, the center for the University of San Francisco, winner of the NCAA basketball tournament, and later the best center ever to play basketball. He played pro for the Boston Celtics and was a defensive specialist. K.C. Jones was with them too. We must have heard some of their games on the radio. Everyone was startled to see them, but it was a nice change.

One Saturday I was out in the yard, sitting up on the top step of the big steps. I was watching the cons just below me playing handball, looking up to the other end of the yard where they were playing baseball, and watching some of the cons walking up and down between the two activities. I was also looking at the Golden Gate Bridge.

The wind was blowing from the southwest, San Francisco, and it was a warm sunny day. Then an odor came to me on the wind that shook me to the core. NEW MOWN GRASS! They must have been mowing the grass on the Marina Green. I hadn't smelled new mown grass for years, but I immediately recognized the odor.

Then I asked myself the question, "What am I doing here, when I could be where I could smell the grass?" This question seemed very important to me and the next question was, "Why am I here?" The answer to that was that I had tried to escape from Leavenworth.

And before that I had some disciplinary problems in McNeil Island and I was there because I had helped rob a bank. Before that I was in San Quentin for stealing a car, carrying a gun, and assaulting another prisoner. Before that I had a General Court Martial in the Navy for going AWOL and served a year in Navy prison for assaulting a Marine guard. And before the Navy, I had my juvenile problems, and had left home when I was 15 years old, over my mother's objections and tears.

Then it dawned on me, like I had been hit with a baseball bat to get my attention. That everything I had done to get to this point in my life was BY MY OWN CHOICE. I had chosen to come to Alcatraz! I had actually been moving in the direction to put me in this spot at this time, by my own choice! I was sitting on these steps in Alcatraz looking at the view BY MY OWN CHOICE!

It was an astounding revelation, and it took several minutes to sink in. That instant I realized the truth, that no one was responsible for my actions but me. All the blame I had placed on anybody else was gone. There was no rancor or ill feeling left for anyone but myself. And if, in the end, a person can't forgive himself, who will forgive him?

Then my next thought was what to do about it? I had several more months left of my federal sentence and probably two more years in San Quentin for parole violation. So I reasoned that if I had come to Alcatraz by my own choice, then it was certainly my choice to do the rest of my time, get out of prison, get a job, and go straight. I knew it would be a hard row to hoe, but it was my choice.

It was a choice between life and death, of staying in one of these rat holes the rest of my life or being out where I could smell the grass. I also realized that I no longer felt like I had any connection to the other cons, and that they were just an infestation to get away from. But I knew that I had to keep all these thoughts to myself because if a con thought I was getting soft, they would do something. But this epiphany only made me stronger in my resolution to get out, go straight and make a new life for myself. God help anyone who interfered with that resolve.

I sat there on the yard steps of Alcatraz, looking at the view of San Francisco and the Golden Gate Bridge, knowing that soon I would be over THERE. One thing I couldn't fathom in a thousand years was that in 52 years I would be sitting in the same spot remembering that day when I had my epiphany, and feeling the same emotion. I could swear that while I was sitting there that the wind brought me the smell of new mown grass. Or was the whole Alcatraz experience just a figment of my imagination?

This is like one of the dryers I worked on for four years.

Looking North at the baseball diamond.

1957 - Bill Russell, Guard George DeVincenzi, K.C. Jones,
Lt. Ryehner, Father Scanell

Chapter Five
April 26, 1959
to August 8, 2010

THREE DAYS BEFORE my scheduled release from Alcatraz, Warden Madigan told me that my hold for parole violation from California had been dropped, and that I would be released directly from Alcatraz. I understand now that only five or six prisoners in the history of the prison had been released that way. Usually, they were transferred to a prison near where they were convicted or near where they had family. Not only had California dropped the hold on me, but the state had reduced my sentence to time served, and discharged me from their custody! What a surprise.

The shock of hearing that I was going to be released in three days almost floored me. Then came confusion and a little panic. I had reconciled myself to going back to San Quentin or Folsom for at least two more years. But the confusion lasted only a few minutes, and an immense feeling of joy that I was getting out came over me.

On the morning of April 26, 1959 my cell door opened and I was taken down to the shower room. I was given new shorts, sport shirt, pants, sport coat, socks, and dress shoes. And a release mug shot. The shirt was the ugliest shirt that I had ever seen. But it was a freedom shirt.

Then one guard took me out of the prison through the basement gate. It was the same way I come in over five years before. We got on the little bus and went down the narrow, winding road to the dock. On the way down I could see the tall buildings of downtown San Francisco again, as that view couldn't be seen from the big steps in the recreation yard or the cell house.

The Alcatraz boat—the Warden Johnson—was tied up at the dock, and soonafter we boarded and headed for San Francisco, and the boat dock at Fort Mason. The guard and I got into a nearby car, left Fort Mason, and entered the city. The crowds of people, cars, buses, taxis, and the haste of everyone's movements was unnerving to me. But the colors and immense distances seemed astounding. I had just come from a place that had no color, and the farthest you could walk in one direction was less than 100 yards. The whole experience was really overwhelming.

We arrived at the airport and the guard escorted me onto a passenger jet airplane. I was soon on my way to Los Angeles. The small compartment of the airplane actually calmed my nerves a little; no one seemed to be in such a frantic hurry. I hadn't hurried anywhere for years. No running was allowed in Alcatraz, except in the yard.

After about an hour, the plane landed at John Wayne Airport in Orange County. My uncle John met me at the terminal and drove me to my brother Darwin's house. I stayed there with him and his wife Carol, who was 8 months pregnant, for two months. Their house was in Van Nuys, California. The first thing I did when I got to my brother's house was to sit down on his front lawn! I could smell the grass and it was great! They wondered what was wrong with me. And I explained a little of what had happened in Alcatraz on the recreation yard steps.

The next day my brother took me to downtown Los Angeles and I checked in with my parole officer. He gave me all the do's and don'ts and told me to get a job right away, or even sooner if possible.

I started looking in the paper for some type of work that I could do, as I had no training or experience in anything but robbery, burglary, and beating people up. There were no ads for that.

On the second day I saw a help ad for a warehouse man in an electronics company. That was something I could do, because I was strong and healthy, and only 32 years old. I went down to the place of business and was interviewed by one of the owners. Two brothers owned the firm, Jews, so they knew something about the travails of the downtrodden. I had already made up my mind to be completely honest, as that was to be part of my new way of life. I had come to the conclusion that there was no way I could cover up the last 11 years and my lack of experience and references. The one brother listened and then called his brother into the room, and we went over everything again. They talked it over and decided to give me a chance, and I was hired.

Within two weeks after I started to work I almost blew everything with a loss of temper. One of the employees in the warehouse was very bossy, even though he was not the boss. But he wanted to let the new guy know just where he stood. One day he put his face close to mine and was giving me hell about something I had done wrong. The hard con in me came out and I hit him with a short left hook and he went down in a heap. There were several other employees watching and they were surprised at my sudden explosion. I never have believed in arguing. When someone wanted to argue with me, I would think about the best way to get him on the ground to start kicking him. When he came around, someone had to explain to him what had happened. I never had any trouble there again, and this bossy employee quit trying to be the boss. I was lucky the incident didn't go any further.

I worked there for about four months, bought an old car and got an apartment. My sister-in-law Carol had her baby and named her Cathy. She was born in 1959, so we started our new lives in the same year. I was accepted into my sister-in-law's family and met one of her nieces. Barbara was 19 and knew of my history, as all of her relatives did. We were married in the fall of 1959 at her grandmother's house by a Mormon Bishop. All of her family and mine were present. It was a happy time, even though now I believe, rightly, that some people there had misgivings.

They were right to feel that way, because I was a hardened ex-con, with a hair trigger temper, (somewhat controlled), who had survived for years in an environment of suspicion, paranoia, sullen prisoners, guards, and violence. There was no way they could understand my needs nor could I understand theirs. I will take this opportunity to publicly apologize to Barbara, my son Matthew, and all of our families for any mental harm that I inflicted on them. And to thank all of them for their help.

Shortly after we were married, I talked my way into a job as a waiter in an Italian restaurant. It was simple work and I was surprised to learn that I could get along really well with the customers and the other employees. In about six months I went to work in a top restaurant in Studio City. There I learned to make Caesar salads, carve birds, make other dressings at the table, and to be a top waiter. Matthew was born in 1961 and we soon moved to Bakersfield, California, where my wife's family lived. There was a good French restaurant there and I had no trouble getting a job. It was there that I learned the cart and silver service needed to work in a top French restaurant.

My wife and I were having some problems and it soon became obvious that we didn't understand each other's needs. So after a year I left and went to San Francisco. I checked in at the union and was sent over to a French restaurant (Ernie's), where I worked for two years. Then I went to work in Sausalito at Ondines, another French restaurant, for another year. During this time I played golf, five times a week, which I had taken up within a year after I got out of Alcatraz, It was the grass again! I also really liked to fish. No grass, but being outside was important to me.

I moved back to Bakersfield and my wife and I tried again to make the marriage work. Soon after I returned, my wife's little sister (nine years old) wanted to get on a girls softball team. Sports was a big deal in Bakersfield, and since all kids wanted to be the pitcher, I taught her how to pitch. I think she averaged ten strikeouts a game. Melissa, her parents, Barbara, Matthew and I went to the team tryouts. There were to be eight teams, picked at random. Melissa was picked by a team owned and sponsored by a company owned by Bill Duckett. The first thing he did was to find out who was to be the 'Pitcher'. When Melissa's turn came, he was surprised at her full arm swing and the speed and control she had. He asked her who had taught her, and she pointed me out. Bill came over and introduced himself and told me he needed a coach, which I immediately accepted the position. We worked mostly on hitting the ball. Who cared what bag to throw the ball to from the outfield? All these little girls cared about was hitting the ball, like any youngster. Just get it to first base when it was hit into the infield. I remember one little girl who could only throw the ball about 20 feet, so we made her the second baseman. She fearlessly got in front of every ball hit her way. She would ask me where to stand before every game and I would go out between first and second base and scratch a circle in the dirt for a position. I thoroughly enjoyed the years I coached those teams.

Bill Duckett and I became good friends, and so did our wives, his two children, and Barbara's family. Bill and I played golf, hunted quail and pheasant together, and got along really well.

When I first got back from San Francisco, I wanted

to do some other kind of work. My father-in-law was a drapery installer and made a good living. He offered to teach me that trade. I thought there was nothing much to learn, but I was mistaken, and it took a little time to learn. But I could already get along with people and had no trouble in that respect. Soon I was a very efficient drapery installer, with several accounts of my own.

In the meantime, Barbara and I were growing farther apart. In 1970 we divorced. There wasn't much acrimony and I visited my son often.

I moved back to Los Angeles that year and got a job with a big company that made all the draperies for all the Sears stores in Los Angeles County. I got paid about one dollar a foot and could install about 400 feet a day. Unless there were swags, cornices, or other fancy stuff. I lived with my mother until I found an apartment. I carried my golf clubs and some fishing equipment with me, just in case I had some time in the afternoon.

There was a young lady (about 29 years old) who worked in the office and we slowly became acquainted. In 1973 I finally asked her for a date, and she accepted. Her name was Ida Marie. Our first date was on the 4th of July that year and we started out at Busch Gardens in Van Nuys. Then we went to my apartment in Norwalk to change clothes and went down to the Huntington Beach pier. There was a party fishing boat that went out from the end of the pier twice a day and we took the evening trip starting at 4pm.

The boat went about a mile off shore and on the way out I taught Ida how to cast the spinning reel and how to handle the rod. We stopped near the kelp beds and I used the small net to fish a live anchovy out of the bait tank, showed Ida how to hook it, and told her "you're on your own kid." She caught ten sand bass, the biggest about six pounds and had a great time. About 7:30 the skipper told the eight people aboard that the galley was open, We had some delicious cheese burgers and Ida ate one up without even washing her hands. I told myself after I had seen how she responded to the fishing trip that this was the girl for me! Neither of us eat fish. About 8 o'clock the whole beach lit up with fireworks. It was a perfect day and we have had many others since then.

We were married two months later on September 2, 1973, in the Church of Religious Science in Los Angeles. And immediately after the reception, at my mother's house, we left for our honeymoon. First in Las Vegas and then in a little town of Hatch, Utah. We took our lighter fishing gear for trout. Just for something to do.

A few years earlier my friend Bill Duckett and his wife Gale had bought a motel and restaurant in Hatch. I had been there before and wanted Ida to meet them. They really liked Ida and we all remain friends to this day. Ida and I went up there every chance we got after that, and had a great time.

We lived in Costa Mesa, California. In 1975 we bought a 16 ft boat with a 75 horsepower motor and fished the lakes in San Diego County. We also made several trips out to Catalina Island. We would leave the 22nd Street landing in Long Beach before daylight, put the compass on 180 degrees and hit Avalon right on the nose. There was also two golf courses nearby, so there were plenty of outdoor activities for us.

One night about eight, I arrived home after a hard day, when everything seemed to go wrong. I walked into our condo and told Ida that if I didn't get out of the rat race for a few weeks I was going to go dingy! She agreed and we called Bill Duckett, who had gotten divorced and sold his property in Hatch, Utah and was working at Bullfrog Resort on Lake Powell, Utah. He said to come on up and he would arrange a trailer for us to stay in. The resort was 70 miles from the nearest town, so every one who worked there lived in mobile homes. The National Park Service personnel had houses. It took two days to get to Bullfrog through mostly desolate country, very beautiful in a way. After seeing Bullfrog, which didn't take long, Bill took us on a boat tour of a little of the lake. Lake Powell is 185 miles long, mostly in Utah, but the dam is in Page, Arizona. We made the trip to Rainbow Bridge by boat. That's the easiest way to get there. It's 50 miles from Bullfrog and we saw a few Anasazi Indian Ruins in some side canyons. Very interesting.

After a few days of this, we were talking to the general manager of the resort, and telling him we were sick of the rat race in Los Angeles. He told us that there were jobs for both of us at Bullfrog. Ida and I talked it over and told him we would be back in three weeks.

We went back to Costa Mesa, sold the condo, furniture, and my work van, got our Siamese cat out of the pet hotel, hooked our boat to our pickup truck and headed back to Bullfrog! The employees lived in mobile homes. They were double wides, furnished, and in good condition. The temporary summer employees lived three or four together. They mostly were young people who worked in the ski resorts in Utah and Colorado and the lake resorts in the summer. That way they could ski summer and winter, but they were good workers, and had a good time

We worked hard at Bullfrog, Ida in the main office and me down at the marina. Soon, I was the assistant marina manager, but my main job was to take care of the buoy field, where the resort rented buoy tie ups to the private boats kept at the lake. Some of the yachts were 50 footers. Bullfrog also rented about 80 house-boats that slept up to 12 people. We bought a bass boat in Colorado, and felt like we had been on a two year vacation. We both learned to bass fish there and my first tournament was out of Wahweap Marina down by the Glen Canyon Dam 100 miles south of Bullfrog. But the trip pulling our bass boat was close to 200 miles, as we had to go north, cross a bridge, east and then south on the east side of the lake. Over Glen Canyon Dam to Page, Arizona. There is a hotel at the resort and we really enjoyed the trip. I didn't do very good in the tournament. They were all pros!

Two years to the day after we arrived in Bullfrog, in May 1980 we loaded up and headed for Northern California. Our friend Bill Duckett was the general manager of a resort on Lake Shasta and we stayed with him for a few days, and tried to figure out where we wanted to live and what we wanted to do. We were introduced to the general manager of Bridge Bay Resort on Lake Shasta and with our experience he offered us jobs. We accepted and Ida went to work in the reservation office and I worked at the marina. We did a lot of bass fishing and I learned to fish the lake very well.

After six months and the tourist season was over Ida and I visited her parents in a small town about 50 miles north of San Francisco. Ida's mother wanted to sell her practice, they were both chiropractors, and start teaching. So we moved there in 1980, bought a mobile home and Ida started the work she had gone to chiropractic college for four years to learn. I was 53 and had been out of Alcatraz for 21 years. By then I had mellowed out and was more or less domesticated. I went back into the drapery business and two years later I went to work for a large company that sold memberships to a hunting and fishing club in California, Colorado, and Texas. The company leased private land. And the members could use it in hunting season.

Our days off were spent bass fishing the nearby lakes and especially the Delta, a confluence of several rivers flowing out of the Sierra Mountains. The Delta emptied into the San Francisco Bay and has 1,100 miles of shoreline, made of slews, lakes, and good tides. And great fishing!

My job paid on commission, which worked perfectly with what I really wanted to do. Fish bass tournaments! We bought a RV and I fished tournaments at the Delta, lakes Berryessa, Clear, Shasta, Oroville, Folsom, Comanche, New Mellones and others. Also Lake Mead in Nevada, Elephant Butte in New Mexico, and Roosevelt in Arizona. Most were draw tournaments, but some were teams, and Ida was my partner. We did good as a team and Ida has a lot of trophies in her office.

Ida was the first woman in Northern California to be in a tournament of champions! After that there were a lot of husband-and-wife teams. Of course there were entry fees and prize money.

In 1989 I turned 62 and went on Social Security, just like everybody else who worked for 30 years. I continued fishing tournaments, but far less until 1996, when they became too hard for me, as I had some medical problems. But Ida and I kept fishing and I took up golf again and taught Ida how to play. The fishing ended in 2003 and I played golf three or four times a week, and Ida and I played every Thursday and some Sundays. In 1999 I started working six hours every Saturday as a marshal on a golf course, keeping the players moving and giving whatever help I could. The wheel had turned! That job got me a little free golf and out of the house on Saturdays, as Ida was still working. This year was part time, because of my health and will be my last year working, (2010). Now I spend my days reading, playing online poker, and watching TV. We still play golf once a week.

It's been 51 years since I got out of Alcatraz, and every year has been better. Ida and I have been married 37 years, had a lot of laughs, done and seen a lot together, and are still on our honeymoon. What could be better?

Parole Form No. 18
(Rev. May 1955)

THE UNITED STATES BOARD OF PAROLE
WASHINGTON. D. C.

Certificate of Conditional Release

It having been certified to this board that **Robert Victor Luke**,

now confined in the **U. S. Penitentiary, Alcatraz, California**,

is entitled to **864** days deduction from the maximum term of sentence imposed as provided by

law, and is to be released from this institution under said sentence on **October 5, 1959** ;

and it being provided by Section 4164, Title 18, U.S.C., as amended, that such person shall upon release be treated as if released on parole and continue on parole until expiration of the maximum term or terms of sentence, less 180 days; **August 19, 1961**

It is ordered that said person be released under the conditions set forth on the reverse side of this certificate, and be subject to such conditions until expiration of the maximum term or terms of

sentence, less 180 days, on **August 19, 1961**.

It is to be understood that this certificate in no way lessens the obligation to satisfy payment of any fine included in the sentence; nor will it prevent delivery of said person to authorities of any State otherwise entitled to custody.

Given under the hand and seal of the United States Board of Parole this **26th**

day of **April** , 19**59**.

UNITED STATES BOARD OF PAROLE

Release date advanced by 162 days IGT

By _William K. Jackson_
Parole Executive.

UNITED STATES BOARD OF PAROLE

The above-named prisoner was released on this **26th** day of **April** , 1**9**59 .

Madigan
Warden or Superintendent.

Parole Form No. 12c
March, 1937

us sH

NOTICE OF RELEASE

Case of:

LUKE, Robert Victor _____ 1118-AZ
(Name) UNITED STATES PENITENTIARY (Number)

_____ ALCATRAZ, CALIFORNIA _____
(Institution)

TO: U. S. Probation Officer

533 P. O. Building

Los Angeles 12, Calif.

The above—named person was released* from this institution at

12:45 P.M. o'clock **April 26, 1959** _____. Transportation
(Date)

furnished from _____ **Alcatraz, Calif.** _____.

To _____ **Los Angeles, Calif.** _____.

Via _____ **United Airlines** _____.

Time of arrival at destination: At **52 PM** o'clock **April 26, 1959** _____ X
(Date)

Arrival notice is due in your office not later than three days after

date marked (X).

Amount of gratuity granted _____ $ _____

Other money in personal account _____ $ **277.05**

Total _____ $ **277.05**

Amount of money given in cash _____ $ **65.00**

Balance of money mailed _____ $ **212.05**

Address to which mailed **U. S. P.O. 533 P. O. Bldg. Los Angeles, Calif.**

Instructed to see U. S. Probation Officer en route: Yes : **No**

*Special Instructions:
Regular parole instructions.
Instructed to report to USPO 4-27-59

Parole Adviser:
Name: **Pending**   Parole Officer
Address:

*(If released to other custody, state for what and to whom under "Special
Instructions." Send with completed plan to U. S. Probation Officer. Attach
copy to carbon of certificate sent to Washington.)

FPI INC GRO-12-10-48-30M-2654-6

78

Parole No. 60
(Ed. 7-25-58)   UNITED STATES BOARD OF PAROLE

S U M M A R Y
by
C A S E   A N A L Y S T

Mr. Reed

Name___Robert Victor Luke_____   Number___1118-AZ___   Age___31___

Offense___National Bank Robbery_____   Length of Sentence___9 years___

Eligible for Parole___2-15-56___   Previous Board Action _____Denied_____

Reason for Summary:
  (a) Short-term, eligible_____. (b) Special Progress Report for_____
                        (Month)   (Month)
  (c) Annual Progress Report___Feb. 1959_. (d) Other_____
                        (Month)   (Specify)

COMMENTS:

This man has just about served 6 years of a 9 year sentence for national bank
robbery and will be eligible for mandatory release in June 1959. There is a parole
violation detainer on file by the California Parole Authority. At the age of 16
this man was generally dependent upon his own resources and returned to Los Angeles
early in 1944 following which he became involved in his first legal offense. He
enlisted in the Navy in January of '45 and remained until March of '49 at which time
he received a bad conduct discharge. Subsequently discharge from the Navy subject found
it difficult to adjust to life as a civilian and in September of '49 again became
involved with legal authorities and had been out on parole approximately 4 months
when he was arrested for the present offense. Subject's whole life history is one
of stormy inter-personal relationships and apparently a by-product of parental
rejection and a broken home. He was initially committed to McNeil in February of '53
and transferred to Leavenworth in June of '53. April 1954 he was transferred to
Alcatraz after he had forfeited good time for an escape attempt. Due to his maintain-
ing a clear conduct record at Alcatraz all lost good time has been restored. In view
of his volital temperament and aggressive behavior it appears doubtful that there
has been any basic characteristic change in his personality make-up and what good

CONCLUSION:

  Rec: No change.   A. J. Vodvarka   January 15, 1959
                                   Name of Analyst   Date

The last 51 years has proved that somebody was wrong.

April 26, 1959 — Does Alcatraz change you? You bet it does!

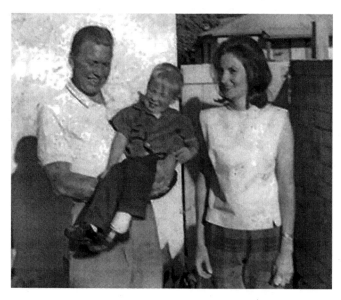

*1963 — Robert, Barbara (wife), and son Matthew Luke
(2 years old). It took a few years to relax and lose the hard con.*

1968 — Robert and Matthew Luke (7 years old).

1968 — Barbara and Matthew with German Shepherds, Big Ben and Lady. They had a litter of five pups. I was the obedience trainer for the Kern County Kennel Club for several years.

1978 — Matthew James Like (16 years old).

1970 — Robert Luke in Norwalk, CA.

1973 — Robert at Bryce Canyon, Utah (46 years old).

1987 — Robert and mother, Beryl (60 years old).

1971 — Brothers Darwin (42), Michael (31), Dean (39), and Robert Luke (44). At our mother's house.

1995 — Robert and Darwin Luke.

*1997 — Best friends, Bill Duckett and wife Janell
and Robert Luke and wife Ida Marie Luke*

*1973 — Robert and Ida get married and go on
honeymoon to Las Vegas and Hatch, Utah.*

1976 — First bass boat, Ranger 1750
w/Robert Luke (49 yrs).

1983 — second Bass boat, Ranger 1850 w/Robert Luke.

1984-1998 — Robert Luke and 10lb largemouth bass.
Caught at Lake Shasta, CA during fishing tournament.

Smallmouth bass caught at Lake Berryessa in tournament.

Another big fish!

1995 — Robert and Ida Luke in their last bass boat, a Ranger 390 at the tournament takeoff at Clear Lake, CA. It was really cold and the sun had just come up. We were last out, but the second day we were first out. We had some great times doing what I liked best. Especially with my fishing buddy!

Chapter Six
Reunion

SOMETIME IN 2006, Ida and I were watching a program on PBS about Alcatraz. They were talking about a yearly reunion and some ex-prisoner was talking about his experiences. We had been thinking about visiting the island for several years, since it had become a National Park, and Ida wanted to see where I had spent over five years. I wondered how Alcatraz looked and how it would affect me to be there again. Being a smart ass, I wanted to go down there and sign a visitor's book with the number 1118AZ. My number. I thought that would be a great joke! I had no idea, of course, that 5,000 tourists a day visited "the Rock", and that the prison had become such a big attraction. Having been a prisoner there, the thought was ludicrous.

In July 2010, I went online to the Golden Gate National Park site, found a web site and sent them an e-mail. I received an e-mail back from Ranger Lori Brosnan who told me to contact Ranger John Cantwell. I called and he contacted me the same day. After about

30 minutes of questions, he wanted some assurance that I really was Robert Victor Luke #1118AZ. And why had I waited 51 years to contact them? I didn't know myself; I felt that part of my life was way behind me. Alcatraz had left me with only bad memories of regimentation and boredom. But I did wonder how it would be to sit on the top step in the recreation yard and look at parts of San Francisco and see the Golden Gate Bridge again. And to perhaps feel the same epiphany I had felt 52 years before.

John Cantwell sent me an invitation, with Ida as my guest, to go the second day of the 76th reunion of the opening of Alcatraz. The ex-guards and their families went on the 7th of August and they and the ex-prisoners went on Sunday, August 8th, along with a lot of other guests. The regular tourists started going out to Alcatraz about 9:30.

They wanted me to make a speech in the mess hall, and that really worried me, because I had never talked to any kind of audience before. I put something together and practiced before Ida a few times.

Never having been to the Alcatraz Cruise's landing before, we arrived about 7:30 and parked almost in front of the entrance. We walked into the lot and approached a young lady who worked for Hornblower Alcatraz Cruises. I informed her who I was and why we were there. She became very friendly and said she was expecting me, showed us where we would depart from and told us that the Rangers and other guests would be arriving soon. We wandered around taking pictures and soon other people started arriving, including Ranger John Cantwell.

The reception was overwhelming and everyone was very cordial. Even the old guards! I had always been ashamed of my years in prison and expected to be shunned by anyone who found out about my past. My wife was also very surprised, since she had kept my secret for more than 37 years. There were very few people who knew, other than my family, some close friends, and my first employers.

I was also introduced to Ranger Al Blank and was told he would be with me all day, as my guide. I wondered why I would need a guide? Very soon I would find out.

About 200 of us boarded the ferry to Alcatraz, and soon we were on our way. The trip took about 15 minutes and as we got closer, I had almost the same emotions as I had 56 years earlier when I was on the Warden Johnson. We debarked and all gathered in a large area near the dock, below some of the guards, living quarters and John Cantwell introduced some of us. We were then given small placards to hang around our necks, telling who and what we were on Alcatraz. Mine said "Robert Luke, Convict." There was only one other ex-prisoner there that day, Darwin Coon #1442AZ. We are all getting old, and we were the only ones that could make it. The crowd of guests started walking up the winding, steep road to the prison, but I took the electric tram, because neither my knees or lungs could have made that climb. It was a far different trip than my first one in 1954.

The tram stopped in almost the same place as the small bus had on my first trip there. We went into the basement of the prison, the same barred gates, and looked at the shower room, which looked the same. We took an elevator to the second floor of the prison to the hospital and had a catered breakfast. There I met more guests, who were all very cordial. The surprises just kept coming!

In about an hour we took the elevator down a floor to the main floor of the prison, and went through the mess hall. Ranger Al Blank unlocked a barred gate to the kitchen and we looked around for a minute.

Then we went out to the main cell house and I got my first look at 'Broadway', and could see the visitors windows down at the other end. By this time there were two boatloads of tourists on the island. I wanted to see my first cell, which was only about 30 feet from the mess hall. When we got there, soon a crowd gathered and Ranger Al Blank told them who I was and that this was my first cell 56 years ago. I was totally astonished by the reaction of these people, even though I was warned what would happen when they found out who I was. They wanted pictures with me and of me, and autographs. I started to understand what it meant to be living history! John Cantwell had told me this would happen, but I had been very skeptical. It's still hard for Ida and me to believe this really happened.

We moved through the cell house and to the library, and we could see up above us my third and last cell in Alcatraz. Still more pictures and autographs.

Our next stop was in D-block, segregation and isolation. I think all the tourists who went through Alcatraz were most impressed by the six cells on the ground floor of D-block. Cells with a solid door and a recessed light that could be turned off. When Ranger

Al Blank told the crowd there who I was, they wanted to know if I had ever been in one of these dark cells, with nothing in them but four walls and a floor. All steel. They were amazed to learn that I had been stripped naked and kept in there for 29 days. Then the explanations started about how anyone could survive the cold, very little food, and especially the toilet facilities. I wondered myself! Some have written that the maximum time a prisoner could be kept confined in the 'hole' was 19 days. Others, that it was 14 days. I am sure that this was not a written rule and that a prisoner could be kept in this dark hole, stripped, for as long as the people in charge wanted. There were certainly no prisoner rights activists holding up placards and marching (swimming) around the prison.

Next was the recreation yard. We went down the steps to the level that was even with the top of the big steps. There was a cable blocking the way. I asked Al if I could go out there on the steps, and he told me I could go any where I wanted to. I stepped over the cable and walked to the same spot where about 52 years earlier I had the epiphany or awakening. I sat down in almost the same place and gazed out at the Golden Gate Bridge, part of San Francisco, Angel Island, and Tiburon in the distance. The wind was blowing from the southwest and I swear I could again smell the new mown grass! What a feeling came over me! I was reliving something that had happened to me 52 years earlier.

I motioned to my wife to join me and she ducked under the cable. When she sat down beside me I am sure she could feel some of what I was going through at that moment. Ida had been taking pictures since we got out of our car and she took several of the view from this position. Then she went down to the yard and took several of me sitting in that position. The look on my face is clear about what I was feeling.

We then went into the mess hall, where I was interviewed by one of the local tv stations. At last the moment came that I dreaded. The speech! I was hooked up to a mike, and a cameraman from the Park Service videotaped the entire proceedings. I talked for about 10 minutes and then took questions. This took almost an hour, as the tourists wanted to know everything about my stay at Alcatraz. Why I was there, and what I had done to get ten years in prison. And what I had done when I got out.

Soon I relaxed and began enjoying the people there. We laughed together and they applauded when I said something they liked. It was quite an experience! Then the pictures and autographs started again. I started asking people where they were from, and they were from all over the United States, England, Ireland, Australia, Hawaii, Japan, Europe, and one couple from Barcelona, Spain.

We then moved to a desk just outside the mess hall, where I sat with a man who had been a guard (John Hernon) when I was incarcerated in Alcatraz. Here we were, two old men, 83 and 88, sitting next to each other, being honestly friendly, and answering questions from the tourists. Who could believe that could happen? But the whole experience was very satisfying, and I believe it finally got me completely out from under the influence of Alcatraz. And perhaps I had finally been really released from a nightmare.

It took two weeks for my wife and I to get over the surprises and emotions of our trip to Alcatraz. And most people I talked to suggested that I write a book. This autobiography seemed to be already written, and was just waiting to be put into words. Within three days I had a rough draft written, with chapters named and the first sentence of each chapter. Then came the ideas for the final two small chapters, and finally the lament at the end. The surprise to me was that after all these years, I was able to put all of this down on paper. I was a month shy of 27 when I became a prisoner on Alcatraz, and a month shy of 32 when I was released. I am now 83 years old and the reunion has opened up a new chapter of my life, and of course, Ida's life as well. And we will take it for what it is, with a grain of salt. A new experience of an old memory. Alcatraz.

8-8-10 We arrived early at the Alcatraz landing in San Francisco. It was a foggy day.

We still didn't know what to expect.

8-8-10 Alcatraz landing. Robert Luke #1118AZ and Darwin Coon #1422AZ. First and only meeting. My first reunion. Darwin's ninth. Darwin Coon passed away Feb 7, 2011. R.I. P.

8-8-10 Alcatraz schedule.

8-8-10 Alcatraz schedule.

8-8-10 Going back to Alcatraz after 51 years.

*8-8-10 Ranger John Cantwell. The welcome was terrific on
the Alcatraz Island landing.*

8-8-10 Ranger Lori Brosnan. Very nice greeting.

8-8-10 Ranger Al Blank. My guide and companion for the day.

8-8-10 Robert Luke with guards George DeVincenzi & Jim Albright, who was the 'Last Guard Out'. For the first time we are on a first name basis.

8-8-10 Robert Luke and guard Patrick Mahoney, who was the skipper of the Warden Johnson, the Alcatraz prison boat.

*Return to Alcatraz. Robert Luke
on second tier, Broadway.*

*Return to Alcatraz. Robert and Ida
Luke on second tier, Broadway.*

Return to Alcatraz. Robert Luke on tier, C-block, in front of last cell across from library. This was known as Park Avenue.

Return to Alcatraz. Robert and Ida Luke on Broadway.

*Return to Alcatraz. Robert Luke and Ranger
John Cantwell standing on Broadway.*

*8-8-10 Robert Luke on the top step of the yard. This is the
same place I was sitting when experiencing the epiphany.*

8-8-10 Remembering.

8-8-10 There was a lot of emotion that day.

8-8-10 View from top step in Alcatraz recreation yard.

Continuing view.

Continuing view.

8-8-10 Convict Robert Luke and guard John Hernon sitting at the cell house desk.

Chapter Seven
Paranoia

I BELIEVE THAT PARANOIA and being paranoid got me through my prison experiences. All convicts must have some paranoia to survive prison. It gives us a warning system that lets us feel tension, and see facial expressions and body language that means danger is near. We can then move aside or get ready to protect ourselves. Or attack, which was my way.

I have talked in this autobiography about some of the violence I was involved in while I was in prison and have come to a conclusion about the cause. I like to laugh and joke, and laugh hardest when the joke is on me. That is real and not a facade. Only when I am startled or feel threatened, (real or imagined), do I immediately become very aggressive, and a violent reaction is my answer to the problem. This behavior was noticed in every prison that I was in, and also in school and at work. And always the report was that I had a 'bad attitude'. But my instant temper and aggression was known everywhere I went and can explain why I was a loner. Who wants to be around an explosion waiting to happen? But the positive side is that I am also one of the first persons to react to any emergency. And I have done so on many occasions.

Paranoia can also turn to fear, and I have seen convicts who don't want to come out of their cells, and even go so far as to ask to be put into protective custody. When they do come out of their cells, they skulk around, and can be dangerous to themselves and others.

I brought this paranoia out of Alcatraz with me, and at first it was very strong, as I questioned every motive for whatever anyone did for me. But gradually as the hard quality of my personality wore off, I started to trust people, and didn't question every move they made. Or what they said. There is still some paranoia in me. But I welcome it for making me more aware of my surroundings. That way I can see more, and appreciate the beauty of the earth. And everything that the universe has provided for us.

Some of that paranoia has worn off on my wife, Ida, and I am glad. Because if we are not aware of what is going on around us, how can we protect ourselves? If we don't protect ourselves, who will? All human beings must have a little paranoia in them, else how could we survive?

Summary

IT HAS BEEN 51 YEARS since I was released from Alcatraz, and I have forgotten most of the five years I was incarcerated there. Most of the events I do remember have been laid out here, but some are just vague memories. The last 51 years of memories have blurred the old ones.

For instance; there were two escape attempts while I was there, and although I remember the events, I have no memory of the convicts involved. There were three convicts involved in two attempts. In 1956, Floyd Wilson #956AZ left his work on the dock and hid in the rocks until he was found. In 1958 Aaron Burgett #991AZ, and Clyde Johnson #864AZ overpowered a guard, tied him up, and went into the water. Johnson was plucked out of the water and Burgett disappeared and his body was found floating in the bay two weeks later. I may have known these men, because of the small prison population, but cannot put names with faces. I always thought that Alcatraz would be very difficult to escape from. But a long sentence can make any prisoner desperate enough to try.

There were a lot of rules and regulations in Alcatraz. The prisoners' lives were completely controlled. When to wake up, be counted, eat, shave, have a haircut or a shower, work, and have the yard time. The rule book we received was long and was meant to be implicitly obeyed. Of course, there has to be a realization that the guards, who enforced these rules, also were completely controlled by this regimen while they worked in the prison. So everyone on Alcatraz had to follow some kind of rules, which was dictated by the very act of keeping control of the prisoners.

So over the years my time spent in Alclatraz has been condensed to several instances that I was either involved in or witnessed. The rest of the time is a blur, and seems to be only a very short moment in my life. Even the memories of loneliness, boredom, and dejection have diminished to the point that they are almost not viable. My time in Alcatraz seems like a bad dream!

Since my return to Alcatraz on August, 8, 2010, one mystery has baffled me. Why couldn't I remember every day that I spent on Alcatraz? Everything about my stay there seemed to be a blur, except for some outstanding happenings. Every one I talked to agreed with me that over the 51 years that I had been out, I had buried the memories so deep that I couldn't remember them. Was Alcatraz Prison so easy to do time in that there were no memories? Or perhaps do I just have a bad memory? On the contrary. I have a very good memory. Every word of this book was written using my memory of the events that happened long before I was in Alcatraz. Also that is true of the years after I was released from Alcatraz. So on June1,2011, 9 months after I returned to Alcatraz, the answer came to me. This answer sounds logical to me.

I spent a total of 1838 days incarcerated in Alcatraz. If 5 days a week were spent exactly the same way, then all I had to remember was one of those days. (1300) The rest were the same. And if I spent every weekend (2 days) the same, that also was one memory. (520) That means the fights, riots, killings, jobs, hospital stay, and any other activity that I have written about in this book are the only memories that I need to remember. That number comes to about 18 days. And as I have written about those memories, then my conclusion is that my memory of Alcatraz is very good after all.

In a normal life outside of prison there are many things to do. We can go to the movies, go out to dinner, go fishing, golfing, or any other activity that interests us. Including taking a trip anywhere in the world. If we can afford it!

Incarceration in any prison afforded the inmate a certain freedom of movement. But Alcatraz allowed none of that, as every aspect of our lives was controlled. So two things happened because of this unnatural control. Boredom and violence. Other than the boredom, the only part of my incarceration that I remember about Alcatraz was conjoined with some type of violence. And I remember all of that.

Does this explanation satisfy any doubt that my memory is intact? Yes it does.

Looking back on the lost 12 years of my life and thinking about the 'could have beens', absolutely becomes a meaningless past time. It's much better to dwell on the 51 post Alcatraz years and to rejoice in that new life. The first 15 years of my life was filled with family, school, church, boy scouts, and sports. The last 51 years have been lived with marriage, work, fishing, golfing, and finally retirement. The 12 years I spent in prison was a little side trip that I took by my own choice. But I did know the difference between right and wrong, and I finally went right.

I don't know why I was sent to Alcatraz. I was not one of the notorious criminals of the 30's or a famous mobster. I was just an average bank robber, burglar, car thief, and assaulter. I did try to escape from Leavenworth and was considered to be an escape risk, and I thought of escaping from a few other prisons. But I was like any person who was ever in prison and wanted nothing more than to be out in the free world and do whatever they wanted. And smell the grass! Instead my choice, and theirs, was to finally be entombed in Alcatraz. Also my choice was to get out and stay out! Even though I have been out of prison for 51 years, the penance continues. There are some things I can never do, and some people I can never become.

I became a prisoner in Alcatraz on April 14, 1954, which is not long after April 1st, and for over five years I waited for someone to call out 'APRIL FOOL'. But no one ever did!

PARADISE!

CPSIA information can be obtained at www.ICGtesting.com
Printed in the USA
LVOW092223200112

264814LV00003B/3/P

9 780578 082950